DERRICK DIXON

Sit Your
Dumb
Ass Down

Sit Your Dumb Ass Down!!

To -
Jennifer
Thank You
Enjoy Your
Book

Sit Your Dumb Ass Down!!

DERRICK DURRELL DIXON

This book is dedicated to Kortez Baker that GOD placed in my life and in my hands...he means the world to me.

–Derrick Dixon

Preface: Angels in the Sky

"God not only sends special angels into our lives, but sometimes he even sends them back again if we forget to take notes the first time!"
–Eileen Elias Freeman

Everyone has a special childhood memory that remains as clear as the day it happened, and I am no different—in that respect anyway. My memory—my very fond memory—was of the very first time I ever boarded and flew on an airplane. I was only thirteen years old at the time with wide, black rim glasses, a broad, disarming smile, and an even wider gaze that soaked in everything around me. Yet, you could never tell me that my vision was limited by adolescence, because Derrick Durrell Dixon *knew it all,* and if you weren't sure if I did, all you had to do was ask me.

I also knew, for more reasons than one, that I was ready to take this trip. This first time flight came from an unexpected event. I was chosen to accompany my grandmother as she traveled from Denver to California. The trip was exciting, but I was just as eager to travel with my grandmother MiMi, because I admired her so much.

She carried herself with a poise and elegance that reminded me of Diana Ross. A set of big, deep, beautiful brown eyes rested inside of a face that did not have one single wrinkle. Her small frame moved with movie star grace as her professionally styled wigs balanced perfectly on top of her head. Of course, she wore the clothes that matched her tasteful demeanor twenty-four hours a day.

Normally she would have been able to fly alone, but this time she was ill. When my family discussed who should be selected to travel with her, the name *Professor* dominated the conversation. See *Professor* was my nickname, because even they knew that I knew it all. As soon as I found out about the trip, I was ready…I was *more* than ready.

The trip would fly us to our destination then allow me to fly back alone. I wore my best suit and felt like I was, for lack of a better noun, *somebody.* I boarded the plane with my scrawny chest stuck out as far as it would *not* go. I felt like the envious eyes of the world were on me, but in all honesty, I really didn't stand out.

As sharply dressed as I was—or thought I was—back then, everyone dressed up when traveling by plane. It was a different era and people flew wearing their Sunday's best. I miss that time and wish that dressing up for flights had remained en vogue, but times change—sometimes for the better and sometimes for the worse.

Come to think of it, when it comes to dressing up for traveling, years later I feel the exact same way. A sense of pride should be taken when a person travels, I think. I love when I see travelers taking extra care in their appearance. Call me old fashioned, but we should return to those days, because when you are traveling, no matter who you are, you're representing something.

Where was I? Oh yes, sitting proudly in my assigned seat.

I settled in for what I was positive would be a memory I would cherish forever. I never felt the slightest anxiety as we ascended into the air in this gigantic construction of shiny metal. I felt excited, but most of all curious. I sat high, craning my long neck to see out of the oval window, ready to spot what actually existed beyond those thick, pure, white clouds.

Even this curiosity wasn't guesswork for the Professor. I had already heard about what was up there. Like most African

American families back in the late seventies, I attended church every single Sunday. During most of those services I would hear dramatic sermons and songs that told stories of heaven and the angels that floated within it. As I waited for the plane to lift off the ground, I was certain that I was about to soar right into heaven and see exactly what the angels were doing up there.

Once we were off of the ground, I kept my eyes locked on the small oval glass window of the giant jet. I looked out it for the entire flight, with my tiny youthful eyes scanning the clouds with rapid eye movement. But instead of being in a deep dream state, I was wide-awake, gleefully bouncing in my seat with the subtle movements.

Of course, I never saw any angels. Not one. That did very little to dampen my spirits though, because I *knew* that they were there. I figured that the angels were just moving out of the way to avoid getting hit by the plane. Still, I somehow knew that they were there with me. I didn't have to see them. I could feel them.

Chapter 1: Hair & Hell Raising

"He's a bully. I love bullies. They have such big, shiny red
buttons to push."
–Carrie Vaughn

Honestly, who really knows what they are getting into when they start a new job or career? We all go to college or into the work industry with optimistic ambitions of making our mark on the world, but are, for the most part, clueless. We dive into our chosen fields that we are so sure will afford us the life we desire, but never even think about the most important question: *Is this something I will enjoy doing for the rest of my life?*

Yet, the lure of the annual salary is the carrot that corporate America dangles. It allows us to feel that being chained to that corner office desk, workbench, or sales counter is worth every single eight-hour shift.

The truth is we don't know what the hell we want out of life. All we can do is pray for guidance and pray even harder that we will pull our heads out of our collective butts long enough to actually listen to what the good Lord is trying to tell us. Heaven knows that I had no idea what I was getting into when I started working for an airline company. To tell you the truth, I can't talk, because I'm sure that my own head was buried when I chose my line of work.

If I didn't already know it all—and before you ask, that little *all knowing* mentality I mentioned had not totally vanished, even in my early twenties—I may have heard God giving me some much needed advice.

"Derrick," he would say from the burning bush—well, virtual flaming screen saver on my computer, but same thing right? Anyway, he would say, "Derrick, you never worked in the general public or in any customer service job. As a matter of a fact, boy, you never even had a job before! Now how in the world do you think that you are ready to take on a job in the airline industry?"

If He did try to tell me that, he was on point. In addition to lack of experience in anything, I was about as fragile as paper-thin glass and just as skinny. I don't even have enough writing energy to list all of the things that would cause me to burst into tears. Just take my word for it—the list is long.

My brittle state may have been the result of things I am not even aware of to this day. I grew up with a mother who would have sent me to school in a plastic protective bubble if she thought she could get away with it. "Sheltered" would have been a drastic understatement.

She, like most mothers, knew me better than anyone. I have to say that she handled me with the care that I didn't even know I needed. Back then, I'm sure I needed it, because during the very few times she did raise her voice at me, I was overcome with sadness.

As for when others yelled at me, my adolescent mind just could not process it. Mean-spirited comments made me withdraw at that time—I repeat, *at that time.* I'm a little different now. This new version of me started long before I even recognized it.

Back in grade school, I recall my first major confrontation. One day, I unintentionally got on the bad side of a little boy who was not happy with me for dancing with his "girlfriend." My guess is that she had no idea that they were an item.

For the record, she was the one who asked me to square dance with her during gym class. Yeah, I know that a few jaws dropped on that one, but back then teachers introduced us to all kinds of dancing. That was my first and last time. Perhaps I have some odd psychological connection with that fateful evening after the square dance. Hell, for all I know that may be why I don't listen to country music to this day.

Anyway, the little boy let me know that I was a marked kid. I sat in the last class of the day, swallowing hard to ease the dryness from my high-pitched vocal cords as I watched the clock tick down to my death sentence. After school I was going to find out exactly what the most dreaded two words in grade school meant. I was told that I was going to get *beat up*.

It occurred to me at that moment that I never had a fight in my life. I had not been in a single scrap and was about to face the infamous *square dance bully*. My mind battled with possible solutions. *Should I run?*

As I walked out to the playground, time slowed down. The air felt thick and it got harder to breath as my heart pounded against my chest. *What in the world am I gonna do?* Then, that internal voice nudged me to use the only weapons I had—my wits and my mouth. I was going to have to convince him that this fight was not what he wanted. It sure as hell was not what I wanted.

I thought, *I can do this*. I grew up talking myself out of anything. After seeing this approach work time after time, I had built up a level of confidence. I got out of more trouble from my parents than I can remember just from talking fast. No, let me take that back, I *thought* I did. Actually, when I look back on those days, my mother wasn't the type to give me a whipping. It turns out that my slick, fast-talking skills were actually a representation of me embracing something I didn't even need.

So, there I go walking into a fight with all of this confidence, but without the slightest idea of what was about to happen to me. I was naïvely about to find out firsthand what a beating consisted of.

I got to the playground, but to me it looked totally different. Instead of seeing the swings and slides all I saw were ropes around a boxing ring. The bully was already there, dancing around, throwing practice air punches. *This fool is crazy!* I thought.

I watched him without the slightest idea of what I was going to do. That was when I decided that I was going to have to follow suit and act just as insane.

"Look!" I said in my squeaky, "If you hit me, it will be the *last* thing that you do."

I may have even been sticking out my chest, but I doubt that anyone could tell. I felt empowered as I stumbled into a realization that I had the most powerful weapons in the world with me the entire time. They got me out of trouble before and they appeared to be working again.

Mike Tyson—who was born the same year as me by the way, no relation—said, "Everyone has a plan 'til they get punched in the mouth."

He was so right. Seconds after those last few defiant words left my mouth, I was hit in it…hard.

My quick-witted, talk-myself-out-of-anything plan flew right out the window. In response, I lost it. What began as an intimidation performance of insanity to make him back off turned into genuine craziness. I gave that kid a wrathful beating. What was hidden inside shocked me more than him. I went into a blind rage so deep that, aside from the verbal assault and black eye I gave to him, I don't remember much.

But I do remember my parting words. "I told you that would be the last thing that you would do," I said, pointing a finger directly at him. "Don't ever mess with me, because you don't know who you messing with." Right after that, I tightened my stomach muscles to make sure I didn't pee on myself.

As I think back on that day, it was a key moment in my life in more ways than one. I stood up for myself, but that was just part of this life lesson. I couldn't help but notice how the transformation from the performance of anger to authentic rage was seamless. At that moment I had an epiphany. *I'm pretty good at this acting thing.*

After that day, I walked a little taller, and yes, stuck my chest out a little further, but this time I think everyone could tell. The other kids gave me a new level of respect after that day and I was never bothered again. The new confidence had more to do with the realization of my acting talent than my Mike Tyson worthy fight.

As we move this story forward, past High School, I naturally returned to my timid, shy self. The square dance bully incident had long been forgotten by the time I started my first year working for the airlines. It still baffled me when people would scream in rage over something that I couldn't control. The airline industry is full of passengers who subscribe to that less than civil approach.

So many passengers embrace *screaming* over *understanding*. I might as well have *God* on my name badge, because they swear that I have domain over the weather, as well as mechanical problems. I was ready to give up on that career path, move back home, and go back to school. Then, somewhere in the recesses of my reserved memory, it hit me. Just like I had done with the bully, I would just fake it 'til I made it the hell away from there and trade the *irate passenger's attitude* with *acting* like I gave a care.

From then on, I decided to use the powers I had in me. Don't get me wrong, I still planned on quitting as soon as possible, but until then I would give each situation my quick wit and sharp tongue. No sense in both the passenger and me being miserable.

Of course, right away, I was tested.

Chapter 2: Hair & Hell Raising– Part Two

One particular night shift required extra attention, due to the bad weather. Flights were delayed and the airport was crowded with people having far more questions than answers. The agents, along with me, scrambled at full speed to get travelers to their connecting and scheduled flights. By the end of the night, we had only two flights to work.

For the most part, people understood the delays. Most were happy just to get on any available flight to get on their way. *Most,* I said. Just when I thought I could finally exhale, here came the person who we have all heard about and, if lucky, have never met. I had the displeasure of crossing paths with the man that the world evolves around.

As much as I would love to, I will never forget this guy. He was a short, white man with a complex that made him lie about this height. Let's just say that the Napoleon complex is not just an apartment building in France. He sported a big 1970s afro with a silver streak down the middle. Hold that thought. You'll need it later.

He was—like everyone else, mind you—trying to get to his destination. Unlike everyone else, he felt as if his *greater than thou* travels took precedence over the peasants that dwelled beneath him. His Dallas flight was about to push back from the gate and he wasn't receptive of that idea.

"Sir," I said. "Your flight is getting pushed back, however another plane is sitting at the next gate."

Heaven knows I tried to maintain eye contact while speaking to him, but I'm sure that my eyes locked on to his silver-streaked afro. He didn't move, so I assumed that he didn't understand the urgency.

"It's leaving in five minutes," I continued. "Just go ahead and get on that plane."

"I was supposed to be on this plane," he insisted. "I want to be on *this* plane!"

"Again," I said, holding my calm, "it's pushed back, but the other plane is leaving in five minutes.*" Four minutes now, due to this dumb conversation,* I thought.

"Hey! I'm a doctor," he said letting the title hang in the air as if *doctor* was the equivalent to *Jesus Christ.* "I'm scheduled to do a surgery," he adds. "I hope you never need someone to help you, because you have a no care attitude."

The mental stopwatch clicked by. Three minutes remained.

"Sir, listen, I'm trying to put you on the plane that is now leaving in three minutes.*" It was actually closer to two.* "That plane will get there at the same time as the other plane."

"I want to talk to a supervisor!" he snapped.

"I am a supervisor."

"Get somebody else down here," he demanded. "Someone that can help me, *now!*"

I reverted back to my intended mindset of the day. *Hell, this job will be in my past soon, so why not practice my God given talent.* Okay, this is the part when I want you to pull out the mental picture of that silver streaked fro I alerted you to.

I picked up the microphone, cleared my throat, and then made a public announcement that the whole airport could hear. "Vidal Sassoon, Vidal Sassoon," I paged with my eyes locked on his hair. "Please, to come to the Dallas gates, ASAP. A passenger needs your help." One minute remained 'til his flight departed. "Help is on the way," I smiled.

In case you were wondering, no, he didn't make the flight. You may have thought that this moment was the highlight of my stint in the airline industry. You couldn't have been more wrong. That was a mere *cherry* on the top of the most hilarious and unbelievable true stories that I witnessed through my time working for the Airlines.

As I recall them, I not only laugh again, but find it hard to believe that I was there. Now I'm about to share these stories with you. I advise you not to read them with liquid in your mouth.

Chapter 3: And You Thought All I Had Was a Tenth Grade Education

"Lawyers should never marry other lawyers. This is called "inbreeding," from which comes idiot children and more lawyers."
–Kip Lurie

I'm not one to stereotype, but I swear I can see them coming. Let me clarify, when I say *them* I mean the passengers whose noses are pointed into the air like self-appointed royalty. They have the same prideful stroll and stoned expression that insist that the airline—along with the rest of the world—is solely here to cater to them. They will assure you that no matter what you have heard, it is, was, and always will be all about them.

Needless to say, I don't subscribe to that way of thinking. The way I see it, you spent money on a ticket—which in return made my profit sharing go up and helped the company provide me with a pay check—so I get it, and thank you. What it does *not* mean, and what I don't get, is you talking to me in any way you please. They have to remember that they work just like me. We all work for a living, so if you own your own business or work in one, you should respect others while they are at their place of employment. That's not too much to ask, right?

On this particular day, I was at the beginning of my shift so I'm ready to provide my *POS*—that means *positive outrages service* for you non-Derrick Dixon followers. When in this mode, I look over a lot of things.

Aside from the positive outlook, I just never know what kind of day a person is having, so I don't take their attitudes personally. So, with my POS in hand, I feel ready, especially since I'm working a flight with only forty-five to fifty passengers. This means that it was going to be fast and easy to work.

The flight was an early morning one, which means that we would get all of our business travelers. They're usually going to meetings or commuting to work. I stood in the aisle with my winning smile, feeling good. Aside from the easy flight, it was payday, so I had a little extra money in my pocket to spend on my overnight stay at our next destination.

Then, like a dark cloud, everything changed. I see this man boarding the plane, bringing the atmosphere down to his short level. He was about in his forties, very clean cut with a preppy outfit, as if his name was *Biff* or *Tad*. But he was not the ultra wealthy kind of country clubber type. He fell more on the nerdy end of the spectrum.

His attire was not the only thing that drew attention. Clamped inside of his small, geeky hands was this big ass package. Since it was wrapped in brown paper, I had no idea what was beneath it.

"Good morning," I said.

Instead of getting the same greeting in return, I received something that was anything but cordial. "Where are you going to put this?" he snaps.

I think this is the part when your psychiatrist says that you are supposed to count to ten. I didn't count to ten and still managed to stay professional. "I'm sorry," I said, altering the smile to my all business professional persona. "That item will not fit in the overhead bins so it will have to be—"

"This is an *expensive* picture and frame," he said, cutting me off. "You need to find somewhere to put it."

"Again, *Sir*," I said, biting my tongue with enough force to sever it. "Your *expensive* picture will not fit in the overhead bins. So, as I was saying, you will need to check it."

"Do you realize how much this picture cost?"

"Why, no I don't. I haven't appraised it."

His eyes dart at me like hot bullets. "For your information this is a five thousand dollar picture! Just put it in a seat. The flight isn't full."

"If you want to do that, you will need to buy an extra seat for your *expensive* picture. My inner monologue said, *If you can afford a five thousand dollar picture, you can afford to buy another seat.*

By this time, passengers are boarding the flight. Anyone within earshot could not help but hear our back and forth banter as they made their way to their seats. His eyes darted toward the other passengers, so I knew it was about to turn into a pride performance. While I was trying to remain professional, he was going to perform for them.

I saw it coming and was ready. Since he was about to perform, I was about to give a show of my own. He may want to say a line or two, but I'm a real actor, so I thought, *pull the curtains whenever you're ready.*

"You can't appreciate good art, because you probably only have a tenth grade education," he said. "And the only job you could get is a flight attendant, because all you have to know how to do here is serve peanuts." His voice got louder, causing the passengers around us to fidget nervously in their seats. "If I don't find something to do with this picture," he said in his best authoritative voice, "I am going to have your job and sue this company, so I suggest you get somebody that can help me. You won't win this one, boy."

Boy?

That should have been the deal breaker, but as miracles would have it, I remained in character. Nothing came out of my mouth at all. A female passenger rushed to the front of the plane to alert the other flight attendant and the captain. I'm assuming that since he was swearing and raising his voice that she thought I needed help. *Really? With this guy? Not at all lady, but thanks anyway.*

The entire plane fell into an uncomfortable silence. The passengers sat frozen, as if they wanted to remain invisible from the brewing chaos. I looked down at him, but my silence was not from intimidation.

The man came up to my chin. I stepped closer to him intentionally invading his space, just as I noticed the captain coming down the aisle. Right behind the captain was an ops agent who also boarded the flight. Out the corner of my eye, I noticed another flight attendant running toward the back.

"Derrick," the captain said. "Is there something wrong? You need help with something?"

"The lady says this guy was cursing at you and causing a scene," the ops agent added.

My eyes remain locked on the eyes of the man in front of me. His stern glare had now transformed into worry as his shoulders sank low. His eyes blinked repeatedly as they skipped from me, to the captain, to the ops agent, then back again.

"I'm sorry, sir," I said to him. "Were you talking to me all this time? I really didn't hear a word you were saying."

His face dropped even lower, then his shoulders 'til it hit the floor of the plane.

I followed his eyes as I turned to the captain, ops agent then back to my preppy dressed passenger. "No, we don't have any problems, do we Sir? The only problem was that the picture frame he has is a little large. We need to check it in, isn't that right, Sir?" I smiled with just a hint of smirk.

"Ye…yeah," he said with a face that appeared like it was on the edge of tears. "We need to check it in."

"And the reason we have to check it in?" I continued, as if I was talking to a child.

"Because you don't have space for it," he finished in a low, defeated voice.

"Very good," I said and almost clapped.

The picture was taken off the plane and checked in. Soon, we were on our way. Halfway through the flight, I stood in the rear of the plane working. I then saw my *expensive* picture-packing passenger heading to the back where I was standing. *Good Lord, what now?*

He approached me and said, "I would like to apologize to you. I'm a defense lawyer and in the fifteen years I've practiced law, I've never lost a case. Today, I lost." He handed me a card and said, "If you ever need a job in law, call me. You're good."

I have always watched Oprah, Dr. Phil, and other talk shows that taught lessons about forgiveness. You know Oprah is always trying to teach us a life lesson, how to be wiser, and how to learn from others. I thought back about one of those shows and how I could apply it to my life. Then I realized that I changed the channel that day, so all I could do was smile and think to myself, *Go sit your dumb ass down.*

Chapter 4: WWDD
(What would Derrick do?)

"It isn't until you come to a spiritual understanding of who you are—not necessarily a religious feeling, but deep down, the spirit within—that you can begin to take control."
—Oprah Winfrey

There are some days that you just know are going to be good. For me, it was always on the days that I knew I was flying with my BFF—or Best Friend Forever for those who may not be up to date on their acronyms. We did something that is called a buddy bid. This not only allowed us to fly together, but also helped us avoid flying with other crazy flight attendants. Even though three flight attendants were required to work the flight, we were fine with that. We were confident that our strong personalities could overpower any third wheel, so they would essentially just be along for the ride.

Before I get into this story, let me tell you a little about my BFF. She is what I call the Black Lucille Ball—dingy as a school bell. She is tall and light skinned with this fire-red hair—ahem, store bought red hair. That's why I call her the Black Lucy.

She once called me from her *home* phone. "Derrick?"

"Yes?" I said.

"Could you do me a favor?

"Sure, what is it?"

"I can't find my cell phone. Will you call it so I can hear it ringing?"

So, I called the cell phone for her. As it was ringing, a thought came to me. *Excuse me, Ding Dong, couldn't you just have called your cell phone from your home phone?*

But that was so typical for my BFF. She may have been a little spacey, but the girl could cook. Every time we would fly together, she would cook these wonderful meals and we would eat like we were at a buffet. We would also invite the third flight attendant to take a bite or two, but seldom three.

The only time I didn't eat well when we flew together was when she was mad at me. On those days, she would bring cheese, sour cream, and things like that, because she knew I was allergic to dairy products. *Heifer!* But we always kissed and made up. Before long, we were back to flying together again.

One day, our third wheel just happened to be this little Jewish guy. He was an ex-priest turned flight attendant—file that under something you don't see everyday. On the positive side, if I needed some kind of prayer—and Lord knows I do sometimes—I had him along for a few Hail Mary's.

As third wheels go, he was a good one. He had this true, New York accent, was of short statue, and had thick, jet-black hair. My BFF and I just fell in love with him. We really enjoyed flying with him far more than most of the others. Needless to say, we fed him too, until one fateful flight.

We were on our way to Salt Lake City. We had two more hours before we were set to land and everything was going smoothly. I was working in the back, my BFF was taking care of the front, and the ex-priest covered the mid cabin. All of a sudden, the call button goes off.

When call buttons are pushed on the plane that means somebody wants something else to drink or have *emergency* trash they want us to take away. Make no mistake, it annoys the hell out of all of us. Just a little public service announcement for you frequent flyers out there.

Anyway, I looked out in the aisle and noticed a lot of movement going on up front. My BFF gave me the universal hand signal to pick up the inter phone in the back.

"Hey, what's going on up front?" I asked.

"Get up here, quick," she said in a panicked voice. "This guy just passed out."

I made my way to the front of the plane in a controlled rush. Once I got there, I took over and assisted the passenger the best way I knew how—thank God for in-flight training. The airline taught us exactly how to handle this type of situation, so instinct kicked in.

The unconscious man was an older black gentleman who had to be in his late eighties. Seeing that he was elderly, I was very cautious. I thought, *Please God, don't let this man die!*

Just like before, my training kicked in to deal with the situation. The first thing we did was call to see if there was a doctor on board. *Jackpot!* We had a doctor. We then got patched into our in-air medical assistant team and they walked us through on what to do for him.

Now the doctor, the in-air team, and I were working hard to assist our passenger. I looked around, wondering where my BFF and the priest were. My BFF, aka Lucy, was serving drinks to the passengers as if that was a priority. *Really, Lucy?* So I swivelled my head around to locate the priest. I just knew for sure that he was somewhere praying and using his all mighty direct connection with God to help the situation.

All of a sudden, I spotted him standing to the far back of us. I told him to come up closer, because I needed him to take down the stats that the doctor was giving me. BFF was still passing out drinks—*God love her*—so the priest was looking for paper and something to write with, but he was gaunt with glazed over eyes.

I showed him he had a piece of paper in his hand and pen in his pocket. He pulled it together enough to begin taking down notes, but told me the doctor was talking too fast. According to him, he couldn't understand what the doctor was saying, so I had to repeat everything back to him. At this point, my passenger was put on oxygen. He had to stay on it until we landed.

The priest, however, was anything but stable. He had gone out of control and started yelling, "Oh my God, what are we going to do?" the ex-priest asked. "Is he okay?"

Now I had my BFF passing out drinks, a passenger on oxygen, and the ex-priest turned flight attendant with emergency training *freaking out* on me. Without taking a moment to even reconsider, I grabbed the priest and slapped the hell out of him. "Snap out of it!"

A dead silence filled the entire plane. Everyone, including my BFF, stood there in suspended disbelief. I could almost here their thoughts: *He just slapped a priest.* I even think the passenger on oxygen woke. He couldn't believe it either.

You would think it was going to only get worse, but it didn't. In the end, it still turned out to be a good day. The plane landed safely and all of the passengers received their drinks and snacks, thanks to my BFF.

The ex-priest turned flight attendant still had his red face, but made it through the remainder of the flight, and the paramedics removed the unconscious passenger from the plane. Later, we found out that he was fine and doing well at the hospital.

At the very end of the day my BFF, the ex-priest turned flight attendant, and I sat at dinner together. I was proud of the day *I* had, but looked at the other two with pitied disbelief. *Amazing*, I thought. I asked each of them how they thought we did today. You know, just a little debriefing.

"I think we did okay," my BFF said.

No surprise there. I figured that she would say that. Then it was the ex-priest's turn to talk. The only thing he could say—with his face still glowing in a deep shade of crimson—was, "I can't believe you slapped the hell out of me."

I looked at him with the words *I'm sorry* balanced on the tip of my tongue. But instead of saying it, I reached over and slapped him again. "And that's for tomorrow!"

Really though, that slap was for my BFF, but I couldn't slap her. My mother taught me well, plus she had the food for the next two days.

Chapter 5: The More I Teach Them, the Dumber I Get

"We confess our bad qualities to others out of fear of appearing naïve or ridiculous by not being aware of them."
–Gerald Brenan

When passengers, or anyone, ask me open-ended questions, I used to get truly irritated. I welcome the questions now with anxious glee. When I say open-ended questions, you know what I mean, right? Stuff like, *Can I do this? Can I do that?* My response, no matter who you are, is always, *I don't know, can you?*

I think I'm pretty straightforward when it comes to that sort of thing. I want you to ask me what you want to know so I can give you a direct and simple answer. But it's never that simple, is it? I just *always* have to be challenged. So, here we go.

One day, a middle aged African American lady came to the rear of the airplane to use the restroom. I stood there with another flight attendant where the galley is located. This also happens to be right next to the restroom. We had both just finished writing down our drink orders from the passengers and were preparing our trays. Once that was complete, we would pass out the snacks and drink orders like we do on every flight.

Queue Ms. Jackson.

Believe me, she didn't look nothing like Janet. (And before I go any further, for you grammar majors out there, I did realize that I used a double negative in that last sentence. Sometimes proper English just doesn't have the same impact.)

"Is somebody in the bathroom?" she asked.

"Yes," I said.

"Can I stand right here and wait for the bathroom to be available?"

You know I wanted to say, *I don't know, can you?* But why did she ask me that? That was way too tempting.

"Well Ma'am, due to security reasons, you really shouldn't be back here while we are preparing the drinks." I lied.

"Why?"

This is gonna be so easy. I looked around as if I was about to disclose the meaning of life. "Nobody can see where we put or take out the sodas. We'll have to close up all the cabinets while you stand in the back until you return to your seat," I said.

She seemed to hang on my every word with understanding expressions of concern. I pressed on. "But since you really have to use the bathroom, we can do this. Turn your back away from us and face the aircraft door until we finish. Then we can allow you to stand back here."

I may have been taking advantage, I know. Ms. Jackson was quick to do as I said and turned her back. I continue to pour my drinks and Ms. Jackson said, "Let me know when you're finished and when I can turn around."

By this time, I was smirking behind her back in disbelief. *Really, lady?* "Okay, I'll let you know," I said.

I left the back, went out to serve my snacks and drinks, and then went through my routine. Honestly, I had totally forgotten about Ms. Jackson. When I came back, she was still standing there, totally still, facing the door. The cabinets were all closed, so I looked at the other flight attendant. "What's up?" I asked. "Why is everything closed up?"

Ms. Jackson was still standing with her back to me.

"I didn't want to leave the area unsecured," the flight attendant said.

Aside from forgetting about Miss Jackson, I had also forgotten that the flight attendant was brand new. But the newness wasn't an excuse. Instead of telling her that I was just kidding, I continued with the fun.

"I'm going to dim the lights a little. If you want them up higher just clap your hands close to the lights like a clapper," I said. I left to pass out another round of drinks. Ms. Jackson swayed back and forth trying not to wet her pants with her back turned to me. I left the back, then I heard it.

Clap! Clap! Clap!

The things people accept astounds me at times. I saw another person making their way down the aisle, so I thought that there was more fun to be had. I finished passing out the drinks then returned to the back with a smile on my face.

Chapter 6: Knock Knock. Who's There?

"I think there's a difference between ditzy and dumb. Dumb is just not knowing. Ditzy is having the courage to ask!"
–Jessica Simpson

Three hours is not a very long time. However, a three-hour flight from Houston to Denver is a *very* long time. In fact, any extended time in the air longer than an hour is way too long for me to be working on a flight. I can admit it—I just don't have the patience. Why? Because after one hour I know somebody is going to ask something stupid. I can feel it in my bones coming on like a bad cold.

The worst thing about working long flights is, of all things, the bathrooms. Having only two bathrooms on the plane is pure hell and the line of people waiting for the bathroom makes that hell even hotter.

I hate to even walk by them. The passengers just stand there looking at you, trying to make small talk. *So, do you like your job? Do you always fly this route? I've always wanted to be a stewardess. What are eating for lunch? Is it good? Do you get scared?* On and on until I want to jump out of the plane, no parachute needed.

Ms. Thomas stood behind three men waiting for the bathroom. She had that schoolteacher look with a tight bun on top of her head and glasses pushed down to the tip of her nose. At this time there was nowhere for me to go, so I made small talk—a hello here and there.

Ms. Thomas gave a short smile every time I looked her way. Her arms were crossed and foot was tapping rapidly as she stood in line. I chose to ignore her. After all, there was nothing that I could do.

I didn't even want to hear the crazy questions. You know, that's something else that just amazing me. Why do passengers ask the flight attendant, "What's taking them so long in the bathroom?"

First off, I don't really care. Second, I don't want to know. What do you want me to do, bang on the door? *Hey, you in there, what's taking so long? What you doing in there?*

Anyway, Ms. Thomas must have read my thoughts. She didn't ask me anything, but just swayed back and forth. Finally a man came out and it was her turn.

The man that exited the bathroom had to be six foot four and at least five hundred pounds. How can I put this? Let's just say that he left the bathroom in the worst way. I can't even go in detail. Just thinking about it makes me sick.

As the man tried getting back to his seat, everybody had to do the Harlem shuffle to clear a path...a wide path. Ms. Thomas let the man squeeze by her, and then after the dance class was over, she looked at me. "Is anybody in there?" she asked.

I looked at her in disbelief. I saw the man come out and so did she. I was positive that she saw him exit the bathroom and walk right past her.

"Is anybody in where?" I asked, now questioning my own sanity.

"In the bathroom," she responded.

That was when I looked for the hidden cameras and Ashton Kutcher running down the aisle laughing hysterically. *Am I being punked?*

Then I thought, *Oh, I get it, this lady might have a vision problem.* I changed gears from my typical sarcasm to being nice. But I quickly realized that this was not a visual issue and changed my mind. She could *not* have missed that guy.

"That's not a bathroom," I said.

"Oh. I thought it was back here," she said, confused. "So what is that?"

"That's a lounge for the business passengers." I lied. "Back there we have a little set up with fruit, rolls, and a better selection of drinks, but there is only room for two to three people, so you have to get your items and hurry out."

"I never knew this was back here," she said in an impressed naïve voice.

"Well, since this is your first time," I added, "I'll let you go inside, but please don't tell anyone that you're traveling with, okay? I don't want to get in trouble."

"Okay." She smiled as if I was about to let her walk past the velvet rope.

"When you go inside, it's going to look like a bathroom," I said, still unable to believe that I was taking it this far and she was falling for it. "Just knock on the mirror three times and the lounge host will let you inside."

The lady entered the bathroom. (Trust me, I really can't make this kind of stuff up.) What do I hear? *Knock, knock, knock.*

Chapter 7: I'm Sexy and I Know It

"Looking good is the best revenge." –Ivana Trump

I'm not a vain person, but I do like to keep up with my appearance. I would like to think that most people want do the same, but whether they actually *do* it is another story. At one point I was beginning to think that I was looking a little too skinny. I decided to counter what I saw as too thin by hitting the gym hard to add some muscle.

By the end of that week I felt as if I had made some strides. I knew I had put in the work, because I could see the tone return to my body. Also, I have to admit that by the week's end I may have lingered in the mirror a little longer the usual when I got dressed for work.

After I finished getting dressed, I jumped into my truck and headed to the airport. I did my sitting-in-the-car-seat dance that we have done whether we admit it of not, while singing "Just Fine" by Mary J. Blige. I could relate to the song, because in my mind I knew I was fine on this day.

The heavy workouts did more for me than boost my ego—I would need the extra energy. I was about to begin a three-day work trip. This was just the first day, and as soon as I got to work I checked in with my positive attitude.

Let's do this, I thought. I immediately met with my crewmembers. Once that was done, I headed down to the plane…okay I was strutting. So what? Anyway, I arrived on board and took the A position, which means that I was assigned as the head flight attendant that day.

The plane took off and I sprang into my routine. This was a quick flight, so we had to get up early to take our drink orders. I rushed down the aisle, moving as fast as possible to get my orders finished on time.

About thirty minutes into the trip I arrived at row seven. Seated in this row on the aisle seat was an elderly Asian man who was settled in the seat with the small statue of a child. He had a gentle smile and was dressed in a tailor-fitted suit, perfectly shined shoes, and a silk tie.

"Would you like something to drink?" I asked.

"Oran ju," he said in his soft-spoken voice.

"Excuse me?"

"Or-an ju."

"Did you say orange juice?"

"Yes," he bows his head. "Oran ju."

I got it then. With other drink orders still floating in my head I walked away, but heard him speak again behind my back.

"Little ass," he said.

I spun around with a wrinkled forehead and my dark eyes darting out. "What did you say?"

"Little ass," he repeated.

My eyes darted even more from my squinted eyes. I turned away from him then stomped to the front of the plane. My inner conversation ran rampant. *Little ass? What in the world is he talking about? It's not like he is some buffed ass Bruce Lee. Little...I'll be damned, and I have been working out all damn week...*

I made the drinks and slammed them in place. My inner voice became an all out audible mumble. "Little? I can't believe that he even went there. He don't know me."

I tossed the cubes into the glasses with aggressive heavy handed drops. Then it hit me. *Oh hell, he was saying, "little ice."*

Chapter 8: If I Only Had a Brain

"You shouldn't say anything mean about people who can't read. You should write it instead."
—Unknown

I remember an old commercial back in the seventies that said in a haunting voice, "A mind is a terrible thing to waste."

The commercial emphasized the importance of education, but back then the advertisement meant very little to me. As I look back, I understand how the driving force behind the advertisements may have foreseen the type of people that I would be forced to deal with all the time.

This time a young woman—who I guess is about nineteen or so—comes to the back of the plane to use the bathroom. Surely nothing can come of this, right?

She gets to the door but doesn't make an attempt to enter. She just stands there. I see her, so I offer my assistance because that's my job, right?

"What can I help you with?" I asked.

"I need to use the bathroom. Is someone in there?"

I peer at the door, clearly seeing the small display just over the handle indicating that the room is empty.

"It says vacant." I smiled.

She doesn't move.

"What do you need?" I asked, now confused.

"I need to use the bathroom," she said again.

I thought that she didn't hear me the first time, so I repeated my words. "It says *vacant.*" No smile this time.

"What does that mean?" she asked.

With raised eyebrows of disbelief I answer her question with one of my own. "Who are you traveling with?"

"My mother."

"Go ask your mom what vacant means. It's her day to educate you. I've got to get these drinks out." A sarcastic smirk followed my words.

She walks away with heavy, frustrated steps. Just as she left, another woman entered the bathroom. A minute or two later, my young friend returned and tried to open the door.

Her shoulders slump. She pulls on the door again, but it still didn't open. She then turned to me with pleading, puzzled eyes.

I point at the small indicator and smile. "Oh, look! A new word for you to learn...*OCCUPIED*."

Chapter 9: Like Father, Like Son

"Every father should remember that one day his son will follow his example instead of his advice."
–Charles F. Kettering

I am a father myself, so I do understand about the whole farther-son bond. It is undeniably magical and has that certain chemistry that no one can fully understand unless they have actually experienced it. The bond is a lot of things, but idiotic? No, I don't think so.

Case in point was this little incident that happened a few years into my never-a-dull-moment career. Just before the plane taxied away from the gate, this man brought his son to the back. They had similar features and the same poor posture that didn't match the father's overconfident façade.

"Can I show my son the bathroom?" he asked. The question was a mere formality, since I'm sure he knew that I wasn't going to stop him from taking a toilet tour. However, I know what you are thinking: *Here comes Derrick's smart mouth responding to another open-ended question.*

I was tempted for sure, but showed some restraint this time. As much as I wanted to pounce on them with my—so I have been told—sharp tongue, I was nice this time. The father puffed out his fatty chest with swelling pride and added. "It's his first time on a plane."

"Okay," I said, looking at this eighteen-year-old boy. I bit my tongue then said, "Sure."

Proud of me yet? If you are, don't be. This ain't over.

"Isn't this neat, son?" he asked. "Now, watch how I flush it." He pressed the button to flush the toilet as if it was some kind of magic trick.

"So," I said. "This is his first time out in the world? Or out of the house?"

Yeah, I know that I gave you guys the whole father-son bonding sermon and said that I was going to be nice. But come on now, showing him how the toilet flushes?

Anyway I got *go to hell* looks from both of them before they returned to their seats. I know I could have kept the words to myself, but I just *couldn't* do it. Call me weak, but we all fall short, right? I will never forget the look that they gave me, but now that I think about it, I get that look a lot.

Imagine that.

Chapter 10: This Ain't Cheers
(where everybody knows your name)

"Fame means millions of people have the wrong idea of who you are."
–Erica Jong

At times I tend to go against the grain. I get a kick out of throwing people off by reacting differently than how they assume or think I *should* respond. Don't ask me why. I guess some people work out of the box, but in my opinion, I don't think I have ever been in it.

On one flight I was taking drink orders and I saw a famous boxer sitting in the front row. I won't say his name, but let's just say that comedian Tommy Davidson does a hell of a sweet impression of him. "Go ahead, Google it."

Okay, like I said, I was taking drink orders and approached the famous boxer seated next to his bodyguard. "Would you like something to drink?" I asked.

The bodyguard spoke up for both of them. "We both would like a gin and tonic," he said.

"That will be five dollars each," I said.

The bodyguard looked at his client, the famous boxer, and then back at me. "Do you know who this is?" he asked motioning his oversized head at the boxer.

"Oh," I said. "I thought that you two were traveling together. I thought *you* knew him."

"Yes, we are. I know him, but I wanted to know if you knew him."

I looked at the famous boxer with a perplexed expression. "Have we met somewhere?"

"No, we have never met," the boxer answered.

I turned my attention back to the bodyguard. "So, I'm confused," I said, still playing dumb. "How would I know him if we never met?"

"So, you never seen him before?" the bodyguard asked.

I turned back to the boxer. "Have you seen me before?"

"No," he answered.

"You haven't seen me, but you think I've seen you?" I shrugged my shoulders. "Listen, all I want to know is if you want something to drink, and I need five dollars each."

The bodyguard scowled, then blurted out the name of his client. "This is *so-and-so*, the famous boxer!"

"Oh," I said with an expression about as dry as a martini. "Nice to meet you. So you *do* have five dollars, don't you?" They both chose to have water.

Chapter 11: There Are No Dumb Questions...Just Questions That Are Dumb

"My best attribute is knowing when not to answer stupid questions."
—Gina Gershon

Everyday, somewhere a family gets ready to travel, for whatever reason, to a destination across the country. Be it a funeral, vacation, a party, or just to get away. They take the time to make a reservation via online technology, then purchase the tickets. The bags have been packed for the entire week and stacked perfectly by the front door.

Everything is in order. They've double-checked the tickets, checked hotel reservations, and looked at the tickets again. The whole trip has been planned out to the letter with every *t* crossed and every *i* dotted. They have a tight itinerary on what to see, where to eat, and how much money is to be spent.

On the day of the trip, the car is packed, the family is loaded into the car, and a double-check is done to see who has the tickets. Plans were made for the dog, which relative is watching the house, and what neighbor will pick up the mail.

So, this would lead you to a reasonable conclusion—this is a well-educated, middle class family with a knack for organization. Yet, as soon as they arrive at the airport and walk through the glass doors, a secret mist is sprayed on them. It is called the *dumb spray.*

It kicks in like a large dose of Novocain. Nobody knows where the tickets are, who has the tickets, or who was supposed to have the tickets. They fight like untamed animals, because they thought they had the gate, but find out that they are in the wrong area of the airport. They also realize that—after finding the tickets—the time was also incorrect. They have thirty minutes to get to the gate.

Like a scene from an episode of the twilight zone, this well-educated family has become a group of the dumbest and most unorganized people on earth. The mist does not wear off. As soon as they board, the plane they prove the extreme potency of this secret mist.

Here are a few of the questions I get on a daily basis. I also added the heartfelt customer service oriented answers that I gave them. Don't look for these people on Jeopardy, okay?

Q. What body of water is that?
A. A *big* body of water.

Q. What are those circles on the ground?
A. Those are pizza factories.

Q. What is causing all that lightning?
A. It's the plane hitting the clouds. The neutrons from the clouds and plane cause the thunder and lightning.

Q. What are we flying over?
A. The United States.

Q. What are all those lights down there?
A. I think it's an outdoor concert. If you listen close you can hear who is singing.

Q. When are we going to get there?
A. Is someone picking you up? Cause if you told them what time to pick you up that's what time we will be there.

Q. (*Grown man*) Are we flying in the clouds?
A. (*Okay, I could not even give an answer to this one. I just stared, looked him up and down and kept walking.*)

Q. How many planes are in the sky right now?
A. Not sure. Just look out the window and count them as they go by. Let me know and we will announce it.

Q. Are you serving steak and lobster today?
A. If you close your eyes these peanuts can be anything you want them to be.

Q. Where are they loading the bags?
A. Underneath.
Q. So, how do they stay on the plane?
A. Velcro. (*Another time I had to walk away.*)

Chapter 12: This is My Confession

"We confess our little faults to persuade people that we have no large ones."
—François de la Rochefoucauld

Every plane has something in it called the jump seat. It is a small seat located in the front as well as the back of the plane that can fold down from the wall and then be placed back when not in use. The seats are used by the flight attendants to sit in during takeoffs, landings, or in the event of an emergency, such as heavy turbulence.

That is the *intended* use for the seats, but not the actual use. The actual use of the jump seat is to tell all your business. We—the flight attendants—affectionately call the jump seats *the confessional*. When you get into that seat, it's like sitting in front of Oprah. There is something about it that compels you to release all of your secrets.

When I say all, I mean *all*. You will tell who you are sleeping with, had affairs with, who you don't like, who you do like, and half the time—okay all the time—I don't even want to hear the drama. I have my own problems, so God knows that I'm in no mood to hear what is or is not going on in someone else's life.

Like it of not, for the first fifteen minutes of the flight I am stuck. I have to remain strapped into my jump seat with nowhere to go, forced to listen. With that, since I do have a *little* compassion, I also have to act like I care. This is where my acting skills, once again, come into play.

When I am forced to endure these moments, I go through an arrangement of expressions. I present simple nods, toss in a quick smile or two, and every now and then throw in a laugh. I can get away with it sometimes, but I have done it so much that after awhile they catch on and the gig is up. They know that I'm not listening and have no interest in hearing all of the problems that life has bestowed upon them. I'm sure that my dry expression still manages to peek through my nods and smiles, so surely they see *my* pain.

Now, on this particular day, I checked in for my flight and like always, saw the crew that I will be flying with. As soon as I saw the list, I just at at the computer and twisted my mouth into a tight-lipped face of regret. I realized that I as flying with— hold on let me set this up properly, this is where the scary music comes in—*dun dun dunnn*…Candy.

Before I get into the story, let me give you my own confession. Candy is not her real name…okay, yes it is. See what I mean? Even talking about that damn jump seat makes you tell the truth.

The truth is that Candy reminds you of a former runway model. She has a youthful look that managed to remain through her middle age. Her silky white skin is blemish free with just enough makeup to make her appear natural instead of cheap.

Just like her makeup, her hair is also always in place. You can just imagine that she uses the right shampoo and conditioner each and every time. Her uniform looks like it was tailor made and fresh from the best dry cleaners that money can buy. When she strolls by, you can always get a whiff of an exotic perfume that pulls your attention without dominating it.

Her walk is more like an elegant stroll. Her head is held high on thin shoulders that never ever slouch. When she enters any room, heads turn and she greets the stares with her signature, *Yeah-I-know* smile.

I personally think she has that old Hollywood grace about her. Think of someone like Grace Kelly and that would be a step away of how Candy carries herself. I need to add something else here before I go on with this story. I warn you, *please* don't tell her that, or that I said that. I repeat. *please*.

Why? The reason is we all have our flaws. Candy is no exception. Candy *never, ever* shuts up. If you met her, you wouldn't have to read my thoughts on how attractive and classy I think that she is, because she would gladly tell you. Oh, you don't have to ask, she'll tell you anyway. She'll also tell you how she doesn't understand why she's single.

"I'm such a good catch," she has said more times than I can count. "I just don't understand it."

"Really?" I always say, and then nod and smile.

After realizing that I was going to have *Princess* Candy working with me I got—correction, *tried to get*—mentally prepared for the shift. I entered the coffee shop and ordered a tall double espresso coffee with caramel flavor and one equal. I needed to elevate my energy level as high as possible if I planned on keeping up with Candy, otherwise she would wear me out.

After taking a deep breath, I arrived at the gate first. I said a prayer, chanted a little, performed a few yoga moves, and then just sat and meditated. I know you are thinking that all that was a bit much, but trust me, it was not and was *required* when working with Candy. When I opened my eyes, the first thing I saw was Candy swaying in my direction.

Let the stories begin.

Yes, there will be stories. Lots and lots of endless God-take-me-now stories. With Candy, if you just happen to have some stories of your own, you may as well forget about that. Also if you think you are going to beat her to the punch and tell your story first, you may want to toss that dream aside also.

Getting a word in on a Candy-conversation was just half the battle. Say if, by some once-in-a-lifetime chance, you do get a word or two in, she will be sure to outshine anything you say. If you met the governor, she met the president. If you met Gail she met Oprah. If you saw a UFO, she rode in one. You get the picture.

Candy had a new story loaded this time and couldn't wait to get to the confessional. She had to start early, because this was a *big* story. She was going to the Obama inaugural ball and the tickets cost her five hundred dollars. *Didn't she realize that she could have gotten in for free?* Anyway, far be it for me to say anything, but according to her she paid five hundred dollars so she could sit in the VIP section. She bought several different gowns to wear to make the evening as perfect as her makeup.

"I just can't decide which one to wear," she gushed. "I lost some weight, so some of them just didn't show my curves the way they should. Know what I mean?"

I didn't, but nodded anyway. When I looked at the jump seat, it now appeared like an electric chair. Mind you, I've learned all of this before we even had time to sit in the jump seat. The pre-confession was already killing me.

Once we finally finished all the flight attendant duties, we sat in our jump seats. I delayed *that* even as long as I could, but it was time to face Candy. Like a DVR set on pause, Candy started right in where she left off during the pre-flight routine.

"So, I have to choose my gown," she said.

I adjusted myself in the small seat and checked my watch. *Only one minute?* She continued to talk. The one sided dialogue about the gown is the ongoing topic.

"This gown has to be perfect," she said. "Who knows who I will see and meet? This is the *top* of the political circle and I know that I am *first lady* material."

She said *first lady* as if she had not said it before a thousand times. I'm thinking, *First lady material while she is serving peanuts and cokes?* I guess you have to start somewhere.

The story went on and on. She told me who she was going with, what time they were leaving, the pre-party get together, and any and every other detail she could come up with for me. I was surprised that she said pre-party, Candy would never *party*—she does *get-togethers*. I took a twentieth look at my watch. *Get this plane to ten thousand feet please!*

I squirmed again. The jump seat was burning my backside and I could feel the invisible straps lapping around me as time crept along mercilessly. Then, like a miracle from heaven, I heard the most beautiful sound.

DING!

We were now free to move about the cabin on the plane. I as off that jump seat and to the back of the plane in two seconds. I tried to stay as busy as I could during the whole flight. I even took time to talk to passengers. *Now, ya'll know that's not me.* I served extra drinks, peanuts, and even pretzels.

Candy was busy up front, so I felt safe for a while. I still knew that we would be descending any minute, and then I would have to return to the confessional. This was the dreaded thought that entered my head as I heard the sound.

DING!

This time, the sound was not beautiful. It felt ominous, dark, and foreboding. I stuck out my bottom lip and made the long, *dead man walking* drag back to the jump seat. I could already feel my body beginning to slow. My coffee was wearing off.

I tried to look at the positive side. This was almost over, since we were about to land. Soon I would be off the plane and headed to the hotel where I could get away for some *me* time. No passengers, no crazy questions, and no Candy.

But that was later. For now I had to endure the banter of *first lady material* Candy. I strapped into the small seat and braced myself for more stories about gowns. I half listened with my simple nods tossed in with a quick smile or two, and threw in a laugh every now and then.

We finally landed and I jumped up, feeling a sense of relief. She had to stay busy, since it was her job to say goodbye to the passengers.

"Bye bye, now," she said with her beauty queen wave. Each parting passenger was greeted as if they booked the flight just to see her.

I worked myself toward the back to get my things and slip away. I couldn't get too far away, because we still ended up together at the curbside to wait for the hotel shuttle.

However, *thank you, God*, I got another stroke of luck. The pilots were with us, so she chewed their ears off for a while. I must say that I felt their pain. After they had been talking to her for about five minutes, their faces dropped with fatigue. I even saw them look over her head at me with pleading eyes. *Help us please.* I understood their pain, but better them than me.

The captain must have realized that he was going to have to do something to curve the conversation away from Candy. He took the conversation over by pulling out some family pictures. The photos were of two little girls that he and his wife were about to adopt. I could hear him explain that the girls lived in an orphanage in China. His eyes glowed with excitement as he spoke of bringing them to their new home.

Candy looked at the pictures. "What are they smiling for? Don't they live in an orphanage?" she asked.

My mouth dropped right along with the pilots. Candy didn't miss a beat and never realized the tackiness of her words. I couldn't hear the rest of her conversation, but her mouth never stopped moving.

The shuttle finally pulled up and we all piled inside. Normally we all would get together and have dinner as a group. Candy preempted the tradition by informing everyone that she wasn't going to be able to dine with us. See, Candy doesn't eat, she *dines*.

"Can't dine with you guys today," she said. She then took a pause for the collective gasp of disappointment that existed only in her head. "I'm meeting up with my girls and we are going to have some girl time."

At first, I was thankful. Then after a few minutes I thought, *Who is this girl club she's meeting up with? Michelle Obama? Oprah? Heaven knows she tells everything, so how did this slip by?*

She continued talking in the shuttle to her captive audience. We had to hear about the yacht party that she was going to— *I'm sorry, yacht sailing extravaganza.* This was feeling more and more like the jump seat, so I got on the phone while she kept talking. I didn't have anyone I needed to call, I just needed a distraction.

The shuttle pulled up to the hotel. We all jumped off and I am certain that the others—aside from Candy—were feeling as drained as me, but not from the workday, just from Candy.

We got signed in and she reminded us *again* about her dining plans. I got my room key and headed to elevator without waiting wait for the others. I got to my room shut the door take off my clothes and collapsed across the bed. Around five p.m. I got up to go downstairs to get something to eat.

As I entered the hotel's restaurant, I stopped in my tracks. Who did I see? The infamous Candy was seated dining with *her girls.* The way she presented it, I assumed that *her girls* were some high society group. The actual group was nothing more than a bunch of flight attendants that I happened to know.

I approached the table and did my best Wendy Williams impression. "How you doing?" I smiled.

The girls invited me to sit down with them. Candy cut me a look that did not approve of my presence. The first lady material was unraveling by the minute. I may have moved on, but just to spite Candy, I accepted the invitation and joined this dining party.

Before I could laugh, the joke was on me. My head swiveled from girl to girl as I heard the conversations. Word after word, sentence after mindless sentence, the conversation crisscrossed as they talked over one another. I realized that I was seated with a *group* of Candy's.

I order my food to-go. After getting it, I hurried back to my room, relieved to be away from that nightmare. I ate and slept well.

The next morning I had to meet the rest of the group at the shuttle to head back to the airport. The meeting time was five a.m. and all I wanted was two things—coffee and silence.

Candy stepped off the elevator looking refreshed. She plopped down right next to me, flipped her hair, and then turned to me. "So anyways," she begins. "The gown I am getting…"

I kid you not, this damn girl started her conversation *right* where she left off twelve hours ago. So what did I do? I headed to the coffee shop and got myself another large cup to ready myself for another day with Candy. There was just no escaping the first lady of flying.

Chapter 13: In the Event of an Emergency...Pray!

"My life is a series of emergencies."
–Lana Turner

If you have ever flown in your life, or even watched a movie that has an airplane scene in it, you know all about the emergency masks. As flight attendants, our primary job is to ensure the safety of our passengers. Part of this involves doing the emergency demo in which we show passengers how to put on the seat belt, read the safety information card, place on a life vest in the event of a water evacuation, and of course, put on the mask in the event of the loss of cabin pressure.

When the passenger is traveling alone the instructions are simple. If a person is traveling with a small child or someone that will need assistance, the instructions are a little more complicated, so special tutoring is required.

The main thing that has to be remembered is simple: you can't help another before taking care of yourself. This means that you must put your mask on first and then assist the person next to you.

To ensure that this is executed properly, flight attendants walk through the cabin to seek out the special needs passengers. If we see anyone traveling with small children, we have to give them a special demonstration. When I did my walk through on this day, I spotted someone that fell into that special category.

Seated in the second row, two children under the age of twelve years old were traveling alone. They sat by the window and in the middle seats. A petite old lady sat on the aisle seat, and I am not extending the truth when I say that she was old enough to be Betty White's mother.

Regardless of her age, she was seated with the two children. Like anyone else, I had to give her the special instructions.

"In the event the mask comes down," I said, "please put your mask on first, and then assist or make sure the two kids next to you have theirs on."

"Oh, I just sat here," she said. "I don't know them."

I thought that I wasn't being clear enough. Perhaps she didn't understand my information, since she was much older than the typical passenger. I leaned in closer to clarify. "Ma'am, they're traveling alone," I said, motioning toward the children. "If the masks happen to drop in an emergency situation, please make sure you place yours on first, then make sure the kids have theirs on."

She looked at them then back at me. "Well I don't really know them," she said again. "All I said was hi to them, so we're really just meeting."

I took a deep breath. *This really isn't happening right now.* I showed the kids the mask.

"If this masks comes down," I explained, "put it over your nose and mouth okay?"

The little old lady heard this and jumped into the conversation. "You want them to put it on now?" she asked. "I can do that for you."

"Ma'am, this is just a demo. *Only* in emergency," I said.

"So, do you think we're going to have an emergency?" Her wrinkled face twisted with concern.

"No...we don't plan on it," I said.

I looked around to see if someone was close enough to assist all of them. I should have thought of that before, but it took me a second to come up with the idea. I scanned the people seated in the first three rows. The sight was like bingo night at the senior citizens home. No one was under the age of a hundred.

I smiled at the kids, but inside I was praying for them.

God help you kids if you need it, because this geriatric group ain't gonna be able to do it. You had better push the emergency button placed around her neck.

Chapter 14: Simon Says, Take Two Steps Forward?

"The only disability in life is a bad attitude."
–Scott Hamilton

When it comes to sharp tongues, I thought that I reigned supreme. In fact, I felt confident that the title was securely in place until *she* came along and made me wonder if I was going to get dethroned and be forced to relinquish my title. The *she* that I am referring to is Peggy.

And it's not just her sharp words that people find offsetting, she has a physical presence that can be intimidating. She has a tall, thin physic that towers over most of the people she encounters. Her skin is milky white and compliments her blonde hair that reaches down to her knees. But the most striking feature is her icy blue eyes that look as if they are about to pop out of her head.

Imagine a cross between Loretta Lynn and Sissy Spacek and you can get a visual of Peggy's face. Actually, there may be a heavier lean on the Sissy Spacek side, because when I see her I think of the horror movie *Carrie.* In that movie, the main character would glare at you with those bloodcurdling eyes and things would fly across the room. I never saw her make things fly across the room, but I'm convinced that Peggy could do it.

The powers that she displayed openly on a constant basis were not supernatural, but delegated by the airline. She worked as a new supervisor and wore the title on her sleeve like a sheriff's badge. When working on her watch, you could not go to the bathroom without her knowing about it. If she didn't know your whereabouts, God help you or you better have a hand written excuse from the creator Himself for why you were not at your gate or ticket counter position.

Although we were both notorious for our sharp tongues, her ways to deal with situations differed from mine. Her actions lacked the subtly that mine were able to sustain. My words tended to leave passengers with the feeling of not knowing if they had been cursed out, made fun of, or if it was just their imagination. Between you and me, it is rarely their imagination. Peggy, on the other hand, leaves the passengers with little doubt of what occurred.

Once anyone experienced the wrath of Peggy, temper's typically flared to the point of no return. Most would walk away pissed off. As for the people who don't have that luxury, none of us spend more time around Peggy than is absolutely necessary.

Needless to say, she was not the most popular person at work. I even felt sorry for her in a way, due to all of the people that talked behind her back. She appeared to be a loner, but that still didn't tempt me to warm up to her. I fell in with the rest and maintained my distance, never making direct eye contact— I didn't want to turn into stone.

On average, she managed to turn everyone's day into a bad one. One day, the tables turned, and it wasn't a good one for her. She walked into the biggest mess in airline history. Little did we know, history was about to be made.

This day even started off bad. Thick fog fell across the entire area starting at six a.m. and lasted until eight p.m. The whole airport was shut down with not a single flight able to land or leave. Due to the limited viability, the runway, as well as airplanes parked right at the gates, could not be seen in the fog.

The thick mist remained in place and so did the chaos. Peggy worked the gate assigned to the Hawaii flight where one of the many flights was drastically delayed. Four hundred angry passengers wearing their warm weather outfits and brightly colored flowered shirts crowded the gate, anxious to get on with their tropical island vacation.

But who could blame them? I'm sure most of them had been planning for months to hear the ocean splash against the rocks, watch the Hawaiian sunset, and then dance in the warm sands at the endless number of luaus. Their thoughts were endless, but fading fast.

On this day, that's all it was, a sweet vanishing thought. All the flights were being canceled—including the ones to Hawaii. Rebooking four hundred passengers onto other flights was a monumental task. And it wasn't just flights be rebooked, we were also attempting to help with hotels.

Peggy micromanaged all over the place with more attitude than workable plans. The workers—me included—just wanted her to go away, but that was not part of Peggy's personality. She had to have her unneeded input in everything to feel as if she was earning her paycheck.

Although I knew differently, she had to act like she knew what was going on in every department. In other words, she had to play the role to impress the crowd and the gate agents. I wasn't buying it, of course, but I don't think her acting convinced anyone else either.

A lady approached the gate looking like she just rolled in on a motorcycle. She wore a black leather jacket, leather pants, and several ear piercings. The lady—let's call her Susan—demanded updated information.

"When am I going to be able to get on my flight to Hawaii?" she asked in her husky, irritated voice.

"Ma'am, we—" I started before Peggy cut me off.

Peggy made it all too clear with her condescending glare that she didn't think I was qualified to address the irate passenger. She took over. I could see the rage increase in leather clad Susan's beaded eyes.

Peggy either didn't see or care about how Susan's growing anger. "You're not going to be able to get to Hawaii for another two days," Peggy said. Her words were direct, blunt, and final, with the tone of *that's-the-way-it-is-so-deal-with-it.*

"Well then," Susan said, "you got to get me on another airline."

"I don't *have* to do anything," Peggy snapped back. "I'm not mother nature. I can't make the fog go away. What, you think I have a magic wand or something?"

Susan's eyes narrowed. "You better watch your tone and who you're talking to." Her voice had a dark warning tone to it.

"You're right," Peggy said. "There's no more for me to say." Her last words made me take a cautious step away. Susan gritted her teeth and breathed heavily back, but Peggy seemed unmoved and unfazed.

What happened next truly needed to be filmed for a realty TV show. This was as real as it gets.

"How about you come from behind that counter," Susan said.

Now, if I was Peggy, this is the point where I would talk back, get loud, call security, but I would *not* have came from behind that counter, but although we may have similar sharp tongues, I am *not* Peggy. I don't have to wait until an oncoming train hits me before I get out of the way. But, to each his—or in this case, her—own.

Peggy fearlessly marched from around the safety of the counter and out into the open. As she made her way around, Susan pulled her hair back out of her face. I took a step forward this time. *I didn't want to miss anything.*

Susan pulled her sleeves up above her elbows. She took off her dangling earrings one at a time, as if this was as routine as brushing her teeth. Meanwhile, an oblivious Peggy came from around the counter like a moth to a flamethrower.

Before Peggy could get to the far corner, Susan's bare forearm tore through the air like a blaze.

BAM! BOOM! POW!

I could almost see the words flash across the scene, just like in the comic books I read as a kid. Peggy's blonde hair fluttered across her face as she tumbled backward from the blow that connected with her surprised grimace.

We all stood in suspended shock with gaping mouths. I don't know about them, but inside I was laughing hysterically. I felt a sense of pride for Susan for stepping up to the plate that many passengers—as well as employees—had wanted to, but held back.

I didn't expect her to wake up, but eventually she did. Peggy's icy blue eyes blinked repeatedly in an effort to clear the fog that was now not only outside of the airport, but inside of her blonde head. Her head rotated slowly from left to right with a lost look across her flushed face.

We went over to her to make sure she was okay. She wasn't. Her nose looked bent to one side and her eyes appeared to stick out even more than normal.

Susan—poor thing—was escorted away by the Houston Police Department. Personally, my emotions were mixed. I truly felt bad for Peggy, but at the same time so *proud* of Susan. While Susan disappeared around the corner in handcuffs, Peggy was rolled away on a stretcher.

I stifled my desire to laugh out loud as five words popped into my head. *You are the weakest link! Bye bye.*

Chapter 15: Wait for It...Wait for It...

"The secret of patience is doing something else in the meanwhile."
–Unknown

If you know anything about Tampa, Florida, or have been there before, you know that like clockwork between 4:00 p.m. and 5:00 p.m. bad weather hits the city. Rain pours down, and not just light rain, but heavy rain with thick dark clouds, lighting, and thunder. You can set your watch to it.

The crew and myself have been through this more times than you can imagine. We already know that we are going to be delayed due to the weather. We have all of the passengers board the plane as soon as possible then prepare to wait. When the clouds lift and we are cleared for takeoff, we will be ready to push away from the gate and get on our way.

One particular day this happened. Once everyone was on the plane, we were all set, except for one problem—due to the lighting that continued to strike close to the ramp, the ground crew is unable to load bags or fuel the plane. The captain made a P.A. to inform the passengers of the situation.

The announcement was clear, concise, and to the point. I thought that the statement was about as cut and dry as an announcement could be, but I was wrong. Of course, one male passenger had a dumb ass question.

"Excuse me, why are we still sitting here at the gate?" he asked.

"Oh, you must have just missed the P.A. the captain just made about the lighting. They can't put fuel in the plane while it's lighting outside." I said. Then I gave them a half smile. "*You* must have missed all that."

"So, the plane came in with no gas? It was empty?"

"Sir, we have to refuel before *each* departure."

"Why, cause ya'll can't afford to fill it up?"

"Sir, this isn't a Yugo where you can fill up and drive around all day long. It's an *airplane*."

"So how much longer will it be?"

This time I talked as slow as his brain seemed to be working. "When…it…stops…lightning…outside," I said. I tried to hold it together, but he had unknowingly pushed me past my limit. "You know what? Let's do this. Why don't you go outside, stand by the fuel truck, and let us know when you don't see anymore lighting. How about that?"

"Wouldn't that be dangerous?"

I learned something that day—when you are being a smart ass, the person who you are doing it to must encompass just a *modest* amount of intelligence or the insults will just keep flying over their head. I walked away without a parting word on this one. Why waste another good insult?

Chapter 16: September 11

"You can be sure that the American spirit will prevail over this tragedy."
–Colin Powel

September eleventh is a day that none of us will ever forget. The world as we knew it changed forever in a matter of seconds. Whether you worked in the airline industry, as a fire fighter, police officer, or had no job at all, everyone's life was affected in a deep and permanent way.

I remember being on vacation all week leading up to September eleventh. Instead of taking advantage of my flight privileges, I chose to stay at home to just relax. I don't think I stepped out the house at all for the entire week.

The peace and quiet was much needed, as well as a welcomed experience. I flipped through channels all day and even ordered food to be delivered to avoid the need to interrupt my hibernation.

The doorbell rang and I knew who was at the door. My food was being delivered—*I refused to cook that week*. I felt content with my isolation in my own private resort that I called home.

Most would wonder why I didn't go to a real resort—after all, I could fly anywhere in the world if I wanted. Didn't you read some of the earlier stories? When you're on a plane all day, in hotels all week, you just want the sweet sound of *nothing,* so home *is* the resort. The past days had been wonderful, but my vacation was coming to an abrupt end.

In two days it would be September twelfth and my scheduled day to return to work. I didn't look forward to this. I wanted my vacation to go on at least another week. The carriage was about to turn back into a pumpkin. In the next couple of mornings, I would have to be up bright and early. My home would once again be left behind as I returned to the friendly skies.

Next to the last day of my vacation was set aside to run errands. I went to bed early on September tenth, knowing that the next day I would be forced from my pleasant seclusion. I planned on getting up early to complete my delayed tasks.

The next morning—September eleventh—was a dark day. The dimness outside didn't match the time of morning. It is hard for me to fully describe even now, but it somehow felt scripted with a gloomy element about it. I just wrote it off to my lack of enthusiasm of having to return to work the next day.

Aside for the errand run, my routine remained the same that week. I stretched across the couch, watched another taping of *The Price is Right,* followed by *The Young and the Restless* as I leaned hard into the cushions, settling in for a few hours of uninterrupted entertainment.

Just as the show began, the TV screen changed. *The Price is Right* was replaced by a news screen with the words *Special Report* in the center.

This is an ABC news special report.

The interruption cut into my show just before the big wheel was going to be spun. I frowned at first, scowling at the inconvenience, already writing off the report as over hyped news. My body reclined further into the cushions as I drifted in and out of sleep. With my eyes closed, the report still managed to catch my attention.

"An aircraft has just crashed into one of the twin towers," the news voice said.

I didn't move at first, but did hear the report. I lay there thinking, *How did a plane hit the twin towers? It had to be one of those small aircrafts.* More thoughts followed the first. *Why were they flying so low?*

The plan was to remain relaxed with my eyes closed until my show came back on, then I would open my eyes. Soon I realized that my shows were not coming back, so it was a good time to get up and run my errands.

Before leaving, I watched the news just for a bit. *This is depressing. I better just get my day started*, I thought. Once in my car, no music was playing. *Strange.*

Every station talked about the plane crash into the twin towers. The details were sketchy at best. They didn't know what airline it was or how it happened. I turned the radio off and just drove in silence. My thoughts were still the same, small plane. *It's tragic but it happens.*

My first stop was the gas station. Cars lined up at every tank. *Why in the world is it this packed during the middle of the morning?* I went inside, paid for my gas, and noticed everyone at a stand still. Each person's eyes were glued to the television set high on the wall.

I was still clueless to what was really going on around me. My sole focus gripped on running my errands and getting back to my resort for my last day on vacation. I tried to get the attention of the man behind the register.

"Hello, I'm trying to get some gas," I said.

He stared me down with an off put snarl before taking my money for the gas. Not one person inside said a single word or even seemed to notice anything other than the television. After pumping my gas, I realized that I needed a receipt, but decided against it, and then jumped into my car then drove away.

My next stop was the laundry mat. Inside, with my load of clothes, I discovered the same eerie silence. Several people stood like zombies with their eyes locked on the television. I ignored them as I went to the change machine to get quarters, but it was out of order.

I tried to get the attendant's attention and once again got the same look of disgust I received at the gas station. "What? You *really* want quarters?"

That was my final cue. I left the laundry mat to head back to the resort. *I should have never left my island,* I thought.

I walked into my home and stood between the couch and TV. As soon as I turned on the television, I caught the horrific scene live. Another plane had hit the twin towers.

The remote dropped from my hand as I stood there in shock, not knowing what to think, and like the rest of the world, not believing or understanding the situation. Like the others I had encountered during the morning, I was glued to the TV.

An understanding overcame me. The next thing I heard on the news was how a plane had crashed in Washington DC. My phone began ringing, and as I went to answer it the lines went dead.

Many things came to my mind, but I still didn't think that we were under attack. The moment didn't feel real. I even half expected to come out of a deep sleep on the couch with *The Price is Right* back on the television.

That notion vanished as fast as it came to my head. I wasn't sleep at all. We *were* under attack. Now that very isolation that I embraced didn't feel warm anymore. I felt alone. There was no way to communicate with anyone.

What if something else happened? I thought about my co-workers. Were they safe? Were they on one of these planes?

Regardless of what airlines were involved, we all had that unwritten union that made us a part of the same family. The airline industry was like a fraternity and we were all brothers and sisters with a common bond. I prayed for everyone.

Tears filled my eyes. Confusion mixed with a bit of fear surfaced inside of me. Before I realized it, I had watched the TV all day. By 9:00 p.m. I had not eaten a single bite and none of my errands were completed.

I wasn't for sure if I was going to work the next day or the next year. By the time I went to bed, I anticipated making my way to the airport in the morning, wondering what was or wasn't going to be there. I really couldn't sleep, turning the TV on and off to see if there was any new information.

The next morning I got a call from the airport. Just like I had guessed, all flights had been canceled. They instructed me to stay by the phone for updates. In the meantime, the phones began to work again and I called as many family members as I could to let them know that I was safe.

The vast amount of information coming in became too much for me to cope with at one time. I couldn't watch any more television, so I sat in silence and just prayed. When the world found out what happened that day, I wondered just like I am sure that they did. *Was it even safe to fly anymore?*

Questions that had never entered my mind before now came into my head. *Could this happen again? When was it going to happen again?*

Three days went by until the airport finally reopened. I received a call informing me that I was going to work a flight. I shivered as anxiety raced through me at a level that never existed before that day. At first I considered declining.

The moment was a pivotal one and I knew it. The only way to overcome my fear was to face it. The enemy gave the whole country a hard blow, but I wasn't going to let them keep me bound in fear. Before allowing the trepidation to control me, I drove to work.

The airport was barren with an unnatural silence. Things moved slowly but smoothly. The look of concern on everyone's faces was a constant reminder of how the world had changed. Once I boarded the flight, the fear vanished and I was ready to work.

We got a briefing from the captain like no other when we got on board that day. The flight was full and this surprised me.

Just like I willed myself to do, these people got back to their lives. We were the very first flight to leave out of Baltimore Airport that morning.

As the plane was pushed back from the gate, something special happened that day. All of the ramp agents and ground crew stood there and gave us a send off salute. It was as if we were the test flight. I understood and appreciated the fact that we all stood together and an enormous sense of pride filled my soul.

We took off and it was the smoothest ascent into the air that I had ever felt. While in the air, the captain came on the PA. "Ladies and gentlemen, to your left is New York…" he said.

Complete silence followed the announcement. Not one person looked out the window as we flew over New York City. The smoke still bellowed into the air like thick grey sadness. Although I am positive the announcement was made out of habit and to bring a sense of normalcy back, I think he realized what he had said after the fact. Nothing was said for the remainder of the flight until we landed.

That day I treated all my passengers with extra care and concern. The crew watched each others' backs far more than ever before. We remained on edge, so if anybody had made a sudden move on that day, God be with them, because this group was *not*. The entire crew ignored the fear that I'm sure was there by facing it just like I did.

Several of my airline friends stopped working for the airlines after 911. I understood, because it was too much to handle for most. After all, I was one step from calling in myself.

So many people were scared by 911, and there are many stories that will never surface. I know we, as a nation, have thanked the fire fighters and police of New York, but they truly deserve it more than I can ever express. They were heroes and did an incredible job.

This story is one that slipped under the radar. I want to take this time now to thank *all* of the flight attendants and pilots. It took a certain degree of bravery to get on that first flight after the most tragic event in out nation's history. As a flight attendant, our jobs changed overnight, and our collective bond transcended any airline affiliation.

Together we stood and still stand.

Chapter 17: It Takes a Village, Not a Flight Attendant

"If you have a small child traveling with you, secure your mask before assisting with theirs. If you are traveling with two or more small children, decide now which one you love more."
–Unknown

Most of the craziness during the flying process happens before or after the flight. Sometimes the drama appears in mid-flight and in the most unexpected ways. I am just amazed at some of the things I hear or, in this case, am asked by passengers.

A middle-aged lady is sitting toward the front of the plane. Seated next to her is a little five-year-old boy. He was only seated for a few seconds until he wondered off to explore the cabin.

The lady had well groomed hair fixed in a classy, stylish, tight bun. She sat with her legs crossed at the ankles, poised with her *Cosmo* magazine delicately placed across her lap. She was the picture of refinement.

Her little boy did not behave like he had been to finishing school. He moved to the front of the plane, bounced in unoccupied seats, disturbed the other passengers, then started all over again. And not just all over the place but screaming, and moving around the cabin as if he had full run of the place. The woman remained poised, not paying any attention to the hell-raiser. *Happens all the time,* I guessed.

I followed the woman's lead and ignored the little boy. About an hour into the flight the cabin shook just a little. Soon the sign illuminated signaling everyone to get into their seats and secure their belts.

"We are about to go through some turbulence," the pilot announced. "We should be through this little rough patch momentarily, but in the meantime please put on your seatbelts. Thank you."

As I passed by the lady and child, she stopped me.

"Excuse me," she said pointing at the little boy. "Would you tell him to put his seat belt on?"

At first I look around confused. *Is she is talking to me?* "I'm sorry what did you say?" I said.

She sat up straight and repeated the request. "Can you tell him to put his seat belt on?"

I realized that she *did* ask me what I thought. So I intentionally inserted a line of dramatic dialogue. "Good Lord," I said. "Who in the world left this little five year old sitting all by himself next to a stranger?"

"Wait a minute, this is my little boy," she said.

"Oh," I said, knowing that it was her little boy and displaying a look of distaste. "Well then, you tell your child to put his seat belt on." After that I walked away.

Before I could get away she came to me again. "How dare you. You didn't even help me. You just embarrassed me," she said.

"Lady, how dare *you* allow someone else—a stranger—to discipline your child?" I said.

"He wasn't listening to me."

"So if you were driving on the road and little Bobby started to take off his seatbelt, would you pull over to some stranger and say, *Excuse me would you tell my son to put his seat belt on? I think not,*" I said before she had a chance to answer. "Now, the seat belt sign is on right now. Go sit down and make sure you have your seat belt on, and tell little Bobby to buckle up. It's going to be a bumpy ride."

I went one way and I assume she went the other. *God help her.* I think Little Bobby is doing one to ten years now.

Chapter 18: Big Girls Do Cry

"I don't want to be a passenger in my own life."
–Diane Ackerman

Some dates are just infused inside of your head. They remain there to be pulled out at will in full detail simply due to the memory that is attached to it. Mine is October first, 2010. My memory of the day is as clear as the outside weather appeared on that cloudless morning. Baltimore, Maryland ontained that perfect temperature that titters between the summer and the fall. The temptation to walk outside just to breath in the fresh air overwhelmed me.

I felt alive. Not just alive, but happy for no specific reason at all. I truly can't tell you why I felt like this, I guess just due to the fact that God bestowed another day on me. Even the drive to the airport managed to bypass all of the usual hectic traffic. The feeling was as if it was just me and the open highway out in the early morning hours.

I usually took it easy on my commute and maintained a solid fifty-five miles per hour. That day, I was going to chance it and push the envelope for a change allowing the speedometer to ease past fifty-five 'til it hovered at sixty-five miles per hour. This was way out of character for me.

On any other day, I'm the one you hate on the freeway. I will drive in the fast lane going the speed limit. Come to think of it, who determined that was the fast lane anyway? I've never seen a sign that said *Fast Lane Driving Only*. Have you? But I'll rant about the world according to Derrick another time.

So anyway, I was cruising down the highway with Michael Jackson music blasting out of my truck speakers. It was like a private concert and I was so absorbed that I was screaming like a little girl in the front row of a real concert. After noticing cars passing by me with the drivers looking over at me the way I looked at people when I see them walking the streets talking to themselves, I stopped.

Finally, I arrived at the employee parking lot. I grabbed my things, but the Michael Jackson moment had not totally gone away, because I felt like doing the moonwalk to the employee shuttle. Again, I noticed the random eyes on me so I maintained my composure and just walked in a normal manner—earth stroll instead of the moonwalk. I did insert a little prance in my leisured walk, couldn't help that.

I went through my morning preflight routine as soon as I got there. After that, I made my way toward the gate. I could feel the pull of my cheeks from the extended smile even as I boarded the flight to meet my crew. As the day would have it, my crew was a good group with all seasoned flight attendants.

Seasoned is the politically correct word for *old*. But working with an experienced crew is priceless, because I knew that it would be a drama free trip. As I began preparing for the flight, ironically enough, Michael Jackson's lyrics to *Wanna Be Startin' Somethin'* raced through my head. My mood was here to stay and any destination would have been fine with me.

It just so happened that this flight was destined for Boston. This city is a great flight to take in the morning, because I love the outside view. It's the time of year that makes everything appear like a colorful painting.

Operation agents entered to lets us know they were about to start to board the flight. I stood at the front door, getting ready to greet my passengers. My body felt relaxed 'til I felt rumbling on the jet-way followed by heavy pounding footsteps.

The steps were so hard that it was as if a football team was running my way. I turned my back for a second 'til I felt this presence at the aircraft door. I spun around, almost falling backward, as I discover this enormous body filling the entire door entry.

The body belonged to a lady, but not your average lady. This lady was six foot eight, and I kid you not, at least three hundred pounds. Her head extended above the height of the door. This had to be the biggest black female I had ever seen in my life.

Her boobs had to be seventy double D, if there is such a thing. Those things entered the aircraft way before she did like two security guards clearing the way for another person. She ducked as she moved into the aircraft.

Her voice, however, didn't match her size. When she spoke, the tone of her words was as shocking as it was humorous. She spoke with a light cartoonish voice—something like a cross between Betty Boop and Minnie Mouse.

Then there was her hair. She had this short jheri curl sprayed with so much activator that it glistened. For my white friends, activator is a spray used to keep those *curls* looking shiny and curved. Remember, if you invite someone over with a newly fixed jerry curl, whatever you do, don't let them sit on your cloth or suede couch. Then ask them where the time machine is parked. Why not let them sit on your clothed couch? When they leave all that juice will be left behind on your furniture and cannot be removed. If you have a leather couch, you may be okay. It can be wiped off. Enough of the curl lesson, let's get back to the Amazon woman.

After she ducked under the door she stood like a towering giant. Activator dripped down her face, mixed with sweat. She sat down in the front row, taking up two seats.

Once she was settled in, the rest of the passengers board the plane. After every one was seated, the plane pushed back from the gate. I quietly said a prayer with one eye closed and the other on the Amazon. *Dear Lord, get this plane of the ground. I know we are overloaded today.*

Minutes later, we were up and on our way. The flight went smoothly and we landed safely in Boston. As the plane taxied to the terminal, it slowed down just short of the gate. The *please remain seated 'til the pilot indicates otherwise* announcement was just given to everyone. My oversized friend decided that she was going to get up to get her bags out of the overhead bins.

At that exact moment, the plane came to an abrupt stop. The only words that came to me head was, *TIMBER!* The woman's large body descended in slow motion. When she hit the ground, I swear that the plane bounced off the tarmac.

If you recall, I mentioned that I am a part of the experienced crew. We are professional flight attendants and have seen it all. I am sure that you are assuming that I jumped up and helped her to her size thirteen feet. That was where the fun started.

The other flight attendant moved toward her, but I held him back.

"The seat belt sign is still on," I said. "Stay in your seat."

Our large passenger was still stretched out on the floor of the plane. Her dress was up revealing her meaty thighs and one of her size thirteen shoes was halfway down the aisle. The other passengers sat frozen.

"Ma'am, stay right were you are," I said.

I could have rushed over with the other flight attendant to help her, but had my reasons to procrastinate. I really just wanted the other passengers to see what happened when you didn't follow instructions. Besides that, I didn't have a crane.

Her flushed face glowed with embarrassment. I remained seated as if nothing had happened. When we got to the gate, I finally assisted her. I, along with thirty other guys, got her off the floor. I then wiped the floor to remove the activator juice so no one slipped while making their way off the plane.

"I just had an Iyanla Vanzant life lesson today," she said in her high-pitched cartoon voice. She brushed her dress down, straightened out her wide back, and then walked off the plane with her head held high.

That early October day in 2010 became what I considered the best laugh of the year. What began as a perfect day—singing Michael Jackson songs, and enjoying the perfect weather—ended even better.

Chapter 19: I Can See You

"Apparently we love our cell phones, but we hate everyone else's."
–Joe Briggs

One or two can be found on every single flight. When I say *one* or *two,* I mean the self appointed VIP business travelers who are convinced that their phone calls are more important than any federal regulation laws. This time, just one of those VIPs appeared on a flight that I was assigned to. She sat in the front row with an all-business, stern-brow expression.

Her body language said it all. Aside from her conservative dark grey business suit were perched lips, tight eyes—fresh Botox was my guess—and preoccupied attention given to her oversized black purse. She shuffled through it as if looking for the lost keys to the universe.

As we pushed back from the gate, she spotted me looking at her. I was sure that this was not her first time flying, so she knew the routine. She picked up on my distant look of disapproval as her phone cradled against the side of her face. She angled her back away from me as if she was invisible.

I stood from the jump seat and walked over to her. "Ma'am, can you turn off your phone?" I smiled.

She remained angled away. The conversation with whoever was on the other end of the phone continued.

Now I assumed that I was the one who was invisible. "Ma'am, the phone," I said. This time I spoke a little louder.

She turned to me and cupped her hand over one end of the phone. "Oh, it's okay," she began with a patronizing tone. "It's a *government* phone." She shifted her eyes to the side just before the word government. This was done in a matter like I was supposed to say, *Oh my God, I had no idea. Please forgive me!*

That was never going to happen.

"Oh, well," I said, leaning closer, "can you tell the government that you're traveling on a commercial flight right now and the government, who approved the good FAA rules to have phones off during push back, that you are not following them right now?" I drop the smile. "Can you tell the good government that?"

The woman sank lower in her seat. Her eyes cut to the side again, but this time they were less confident, shifting faster from side to side. It was clear that she wanted to crawl under her flotation device.

"Oh, you mean now?" she whispered.

I allowed my smile to return since I saw that we are finally on the same page. "Oh, did I just say that? Yes, I mean now."

Chapter 20: Hooked on Phonics

"Take me drunk, I'm home."
−Unknown

Between you and me, I'm convinced that the term *airhead* came from people who are frequent flyers. Case in point was when a woman stopped me in the aisle with a menu in her hand.

Like most of the passengers, she was much shorter than me. She stared up with these big innocent eyes like a child asking me if Santa Clause was real.

"Sir, what does the T mean on your drink menu?"

"I'm not sure what you mean," I said. I really wasn't being sarcastic this time. I really had no idea what she was talking about.

"It just has a T," she said, pointing at the menu.

"You mean as in the letter T?" I asked.

"Yes. What does that mean?"

"Ma'am, I have to look. I'm not sure," I said.

At this point, I was as curious as she was about the T. My first assumption was that it was just a misprint. I took the menu card and held it out for both of us to see. "Ma'am, show me what you are talking about."

She pointed to the part she was referring to on the menu. Once I saw what she was talking about, I took a moment. I tried to explain as best as I could without letting her hear the cynicism in my words.

"Ma'am, after the T there is an E then A. That spells TEA. A tea is a drink which can be served hot or cold, and we only serve it hot."

I'll give her the benefit of the doubt and assume that she had a few *Long Island Ice Teas* before the flight. Perhaps that was the T she was hoping to order.

Chapter 21: Help, My Brain Needs Oxygen...I Can't Think

"If you don't want a sarcastic answer, don't ask a stupid question..."
−Unknown

I try to be patient with first time travelers. I can understand that they have a need to ask me endless questions. The fact is, they just want to talk. However, when they come on the plane with their business suit on, and tell me, "I fly all the time. Matter of fact, I fly more than you do," the game has changed.

Okay buddy, you fly more than me, the world traveler, you have seen it all, done it all, and wrote the book. If so, why do they still continue to ask me these questions at thirty-five thousand feet in the air?

Q. Where are the lines that separate the states?
A. They got washed away in the rain.

Q. Why isn't the moon moving?
A. We stopped so you could get a good picture.

Q. What caused the bad weather today?
A. Do I look like Al Roker?

Q. Did the captain get a good sleep last night?
A. I don't know. We didn't sleep together...at least not last
   night.

Q. Can you smoke anywhere on the plane?
A. Yes, on the wing. If you can light it, you can smoke it.

Q. Do ya'll show movies on the plane?
A. Yes! If you could just step out on the wing, we can all watch *Gone with the Wind.*

Q. Where are we? What lake is that?
A. (*because I don't know*) The Mississippi.
Q. I thought that was a river.
A. Oh, well, that must be its cousin then.

Questions I couldn't believe myself....

Q. Can you open the window?
Q. Can you turn down the engine because they're too noisy?
Q. Can you ask the pilot to please stop the turbulence?
Q. Do you have a playroom for children?

I want to have enough faith in humanity to believe that some of these questions were asked as a playful joke because it's seriously disturbing to think that anyone could ask one of these questions as if it was legitimate.

Chapter 22: Let My People Fly

"Families are like fudge, mostly sweet with a few nuts."
–Unknown

Being an African American male makes me notice and appreciate certain things that others may not notice. One thing that makes me proud to see is my people—black folks—flying the friendly skies. We have every opportunity right in the palms of our hands. We should take advantage of them—all of them.

The sky is the limit now for African Americans. We can be the President of the United States, the head of major corporations, or owners of our own businesses. We are gold medal winners, writers, actors—I could go on and on—and we can also *fly*.

I've always wondered why more African Americans don't fly as much as other nationalities. It's not that we can't afford it, so it's always puzzled me. *Watch what you wonder about.*

Just when you thought it is was safe to fly, here entered the Evans and Reynolds family reunion. I was tired, because it was one of those flights that lasted all day. I was just ready for it to be done and had one leg to fly before we arrived in Tampa.

My happy place was now my hotel room. I'm not one to drink, but tonight I felt like a glass of red wine. With a big glass next to me on the nightstand, a fluffy bed and pillow, the remote, and a nice salad—of course brought to me via room service—my happy place would be in full effect.

As I stood at the front of the plane, daydreaming time eased along. I daydreamed about a nice hot shower to get this airplane smell off of me. When I heard the sound of the voice coming from the jet way, my peaceful bubble popped.

All of a sudden, I saw these bright orange neon t-shirts. *Okay, first off my people, why do we always have to pick the loudest colors possible when we are traveling like an entourage from an eighties rap group?*

The women that boarded the flight had freshly braided hair. Those braids were so tight that their eyes were almost pulled back to their ears. Everyone one of them tapped the top of their heads in an effort to alleviate the itching. They couldn't scratch of course, because it would have messed up the braids. Poor girls.

There were others in the same party with equally distracting heads and attire. These women got on the plane with scarves wrapped to perfection. They, I assumed, were waiting to actually *comb* their heads when the landing wheels hit the ground.

As the family boarded, I watched in awe. This was without a doubt the first time they had flown on a plane. How did I know? Glad you asked.

First of all, I received looks of total shock. I could read it in their eyes that they could not believe that a brother stood to greet them as they boarded the plane.

Once I greeted my cousins—that's just something we say, we're not actually related—they asked me questions...loud, ghetto questions. The questions were loud enough that the people in the back of the plane could hear them.

"So, are you da pilot? You gonna be flying us today?" one said.

"No ma'am, I'm the flight attendant. I'll be serving you," I said. Under my breath I mumbled. Just go sit your behind down. Right behind her another dramatic entrance. "Oh, lawd Jesus, I'm so scared right now," she said way too loudly. She then stopped in the center of the entrance and held on to the interior frame with one of her chunky hands. "I think I'm getting dizzy, girl. Do ya'll serve liquor on this plane? I may need a forty to rest my nerves."

I managed to hold an uncomfortable smile. *Remember, you're proud to see your people flying.*

A shiny, wide grin popped in behind her and moved in my direction. This dude had tons of silver in his mouth, and not braces. He had to be the reason why there had been a hold up in the security checkpoint. His mouth must have triggered the alarm over and over, but his mouth was just the beginning. His outfit had a lot of room for improvement. His pants hung low...too low. They were almost down below his butt revealing—I kid you not— Sponge Bob cartoon underwear.

He greeted me first. "What up, dawg? Yo, how fast this mug gonna go?" he said.

"Really fast," I replied.

"Yo, that's what I'm talking bout. Let's take this *beep beep beep beep beep* plane to the sky, yo."

His girlfriend emerged behind him to push him inside of the plane. "Fool, get on the plane and sit your dumb ass down," she said.

I stopped and thought about what she said. I liked the sound of that. *Sit your dumb ass down* had a certain ring to it.

They walked to their seats, representing the last of their small, but loud, group. The family had finally all boarded up and the "party" was about to start.

The family wasted little time in making themselves known to the other far more *civil* passengers. They talked back and forth across the aisle at each other. Note I said *at* each not *to* one another.

The thunderous, unnecessarily loud, voices, I must say, were not the only unpleasant distractions. The choice of words was enough to make you cover your little kid's virgin ears.

I did get a guilty pleasure out of the entire scene. It was funny seeing the white people sitting around my cousins. They remained stiff as they clutched their bags tightly against their chests.

Okay, I have to admit, even I checked my wallet a couple of times too, but that's not the point. Aside from their less than appropriate language, they amazed me with the ironic behavior.

Now remember, I just told you that they were cussing like Ike Turner, right? All of a sudden I hear this, "Dear Lord, we give you all the praise and the glory! Thank you for this day and give us traveling grace and mercy, amen."

Then I hear silver mouth say, "Now get this mutha *beep beep beep* off the mutha *beep beep beep* ground.

Every white person on the plane had the same anxious expression that said, *Please, help me.*

This was a one hour and forty-five minute flight. I already knew that it was going to feel a lot longer. As we arrived at our cruise elevation portion of the flight, we got ready to start our drink service.

As I began my routine, I got a whiff of this smell. I couldn't really recognize the odor, but it was strong. I looked back at my *cousins* and they had a spread of ribs, chicken, greens, cornbread, rice pudding, and sweet potato pie. They ate like the Klumps at the last supper. I sighed with frustration knowing that they were about to begin pushing the call button. They were all licking their lips, so I was certain that drinks were going to be ordered next.

I jumped into action before they had a chance. When I got to them I tried to remain professional.

"What would you like to drink?" I asked.

I used my overly proper voice. As for why I did this, I have no idea, but I guess it was my unconscious attempt to balance the unruly with a bigger dose of proper etiquette. Truth is that there was not enough proper etiquette in the world to balance this group.

The first question tore me completely away from keeping close to composed.

"Do you have Kool-Aid?" one asked.

I wanted to drop dead right there and then. *Lor,d take me now!* I could not have heard that right. No, my cousins did not just asking me for some *Kool-Aid.*

"No," I managed to say.

"What kind of soda pop you got?"

I took a breath and them let them know their choices. I explained everything very clearly and precisely. "We only have coke products."

"So, ya'll ain't got no cream soda?"

Lord Jesus, again, take me now!

Then, out of desperation, I tried to negotiate with my Savior. I silently prayed, *Please, just land this plane and I promise I'll be nice from here on out.*

Then silver mouth yelled out his order. "Yo," he said. "Can I get sum henny and a Old English?"

After what felt like a lifetime, it finally ended. As soon as everyone ate and had their drinks, all I could hear was snoring. The sound, I must say, was nothing short of beautiful. The white people relaxed their stiff positions and soon they even dared to venture out to move gingerly around the plane.

When the pilot made the P.A. that we were in our final decent, the group came back to life. Scarves flew off several heads at the same time. Wraps were being combed out, make-up was being applied, and silver mouth displayed his shiny grin.

I looked out at this entire scene and a smile formed across my face. Regardless of all the antics, the hair, the bright orange neon shirts, and the language issues, this was my family...my cousins.

A little bit of me dwelled in them and little of them in me. I was proud to see my family traveling—not just traveling but traveling *together*. It was going to be moment in their lifetimes they would never forget and would talk about for the years to come. I was proud, because my family was real and being who they were. Period.

But. I do need to say something to my family. If you ever get on another plane again and ask for some Kool-Aid or cream soda, I will have to revoke your travel privileges. Who in the hell serves Kool-Aid and cream soda? I may have to blame all of this on the movie *Soul Plane,* but please, stop watching the movies and get out the house more.

Anyway, they told me something even funnier than the flight. The family said that they were on the way to their first cruise. God bless that cruise ship. Have fun, cousins!

Chapter 23: A Day in the Life

"Today was a good day."
–Ice Cube

We all have our humorous days. I know I have told a lot of stories about me personal random moments that occurred while flying the friendly skies. With that being said, I bet you're *thinking, Funny, yes, but aren't you just pulling out a few incidents from a long career?*

I can assure you that uneventful days for me are few and far between. I would have a hard time coming up with a shift where everything went smoothly with no surprises. So let me spin off a day in the life of Derrick, your friendly flight attendant.

One morning, this lady on the plane mentioned to me that she flies all the time. "I'm also a wrestler," she adds. "But I am so scared of flying. I hate to fly."

Her mouth was moving a mile a minute. I guess her nerves made her talk to ease the anxiety, but it was not working. She continued to talk, and talk, and talk. Her conversation poured out to anyone who would or wouldn't listen. When she ran out of reluctant listeners, she turned back to me before I could slip away. "You're so calm and laid back. How do you do it?"

I moved closer then knelt down next to her. "This is the secret," I whispered. "Just close your mouth and say nothing. It works all the time."

After that flight landed, I was at the airport minding my business. I was getting ready to work the next flight, still grinning at the words I said to the talkative female wrestler. A lady camed up to me speaking Spanish.

"I don't speak Spanish," I said, giving her an apologetic smile. I remembered singing an Enrique Iglesias song that morning, so perhaps I was looking a little Latino that day.

"You need to learn your language," she snapped. "Stop denying your heritage. You Puerto Ricans think you so much better than everybody else." She then stomped off.

Lucky for her I went to church the day before. As far as I know, I don't have any Puerto Rican blood in me, but a lot of African American.

My black heritage was about to let her have it and about to go into a language that I am sure she had *never* been exposed to before—at least not in the way I was about to deliver it. By that evening, I had moved passed the incident.

Just when I thought it was safe to keep my comments in check, a supervisor gave me this letter. The letter was from a disgruntled passenger. Yes, you guessed it, the letter was about me.

"I will need your reply on this," the supervisor said.

I took the letter and read it. And I quote;

"We pre-boarded the flight and the flight attendant did not help me and my family find seats."

After reading this first line I thought, *Okay, they did say that they pre-boarded right? Shouldn't there have been a lot of empty seats?*

"He was rude! He also didn't seem to care. The flight attendants name was Derek." Unquote.

I handed the letter back to the supervisor.

"This letter is inaccurate," I said. "My name is spelled D-E-R-R-I-C-K."

Anyway, that is just a typical day in the life of Derrick.

If I piss you off, make sure you spell my name right.

Chapter 24: AARP Club

"I'll tell ya how to stay young; hang around older people."
–Bob Hope

Growing up—or I guess I should say once I was able to date—I always had an attraction toward older women. Older women, to me anyway, had so much grace, poise, intelligence, and were for the most part drama free. But what did I know? I was only seventeen years old when I went out on my first real date.

So, true to my taste at that tender age of seventeen, she was twenty-two years old. Now that I think about it, what did a twenty-two year old want with a seventeen year old boy? Hell, I was seventeen and didn't even want a seventeen year old.

Anyway, I remember my first date as if it happened yesterday. Her name was Nette. Okay, truthfully it wasn't a real date. I just went over to her house with her younger brother to watch the world premiere of Michael Jackson's "Thriller" video. Back then, this was a big deal.

Her brother and I danced all night to "Thriller" while Nette watched us. I was trying so hard to show off with my M.J. dance moves hoping it would somehow impress her. To my surprise and delight, it worked.

When she drove me home—yes she drove me, because I had no car yet—I had no idea what to expect. We pulled up into my driveway and she asked me for a kiss. I was more than willing, but I didn't kiss her, she kissed me—and boy could she kiss.

It was one of those kisses where I didn't want to wipe my mouth off for days. Later on, I gave in and wiped the kiss away. The memory of it, however, remained fully in tact. Anyway, I figured I would get another one, because after that day it was official. We were an item. My first older woman and I was in love.

We did everything together. She picked me up from school and all the guys looked on with wonder and envious mumblings. They couldn't stop staring when she pulled up in her black Trans Am.

What really got to the onlookers was what she would do next. When she stopped the car she would slide over to let me drive off. You couldn't tell me that the sky was blue and the sun rose in the east, I had all the answers then. Ever since Nette, older women were ideal for me.

My preference remained that way until I got older myself. I realized something. When I got older, the women got older. I couldn't help but wonder when, and if, there was going to be a cut off point. Seventy? Eighty? When would it end?

If I got to that point, it might even go full circle. It would be my turn to pick them up and drive them around—to doctor appointments, bingo, shuffle board, and yes, the AARP meetings. I had to change my way of thinking.

Right about that time was when I met Ms. Eden. It was as if she knew what I was thinking about giving up on older women and she was not going to have it.

She was on my flight, seventy-five years old, and on her way to New York. It became all too clear that she wanted a young black man to take home. I became her potential victim, or target, however you want to look at it.

Ms. Eden had this stylish flare about her. She was dressed head to toe in everything designer and wore it like she was born in it. My guess is that she was actually born in it, in that old money sort of way.

She boarded the plane with a cane, so I assisted her to her seat. I placed her bag into the overhead compartment and helped her put on her seatbelt.

"Oh, thank you, young man." She smiled.

She then rubbed my face in a warm and affectionate way.

"No problem." I smiled back.

I returned to my post and greeted the rest of the passengers. In the back of my mind, I thought about the way Ms. Eden had rubbed my face. It wasn't a normal rub. There was something *too* friendly about it.

I then noticed Ms. Eden out the corner of my eye. She was sticking her neck out in the aisle, smiling and making a hand signal. I turned around to see what she was talking about, but nothing was there. When I turned a full circle she gave me a thumbs up.

Was Ms. Eden checking out my butt? When I figured out what she was doing, I could not believe it. *You got to be kidding me*, I thought. Okay, let me stop lying…I sort of blushed.

There was work that needed to be done, so I got over the flattering moment. The moment, mind you, that I thought that I should *not* have been flattered with. I was doing my drink service and ended up right back at Ms. Eden's row.

I gave her the white wine and a black coffee that she ordered from me. Let me repeat, *white wine and black coffee.*

With my drink tray in front of me I went over my orders, but couldn't see below my waist. All of a sudden I felt someone brushing on my crotch. It was not my imagination. The other passenger-witnesses' bucked eyes were enough to tell me that they saw the whole thing. A few of them laughed with their heads down. Before I had a chance to deny it, I felt it again. I looked over at the enormous grin on Ms. Eden's face.

"Excuse me," a voice said.

A little boy stood there. I had no idea that I had blocked his way as he was trying to go to the bathroom. I felt relieved it wasn't Ms. Eden and I let the little boy pass by me. I kept going on with my duties. Then it was time for round two with my drink service.

Again, I returned to Ms. Eden and again I felt a brush on my crotch. *Okay, I know this little boy don't have to go to the bathroom again.* I look down. There was no little boy.

"It worked the first time when I was trying to get your attention," Ms. Eden said. "I thought I would do it again. I would love to take you home and wear you out."

At this point I was at a very rare lost for words. *Did this seventy-five year old woman really just say this to me?* But she was not finished. She leaned over and told the lady sitting next to her more of her thoughts.

"He's a sexy black man," she said. She allowed her eyes to drift to my crotch. "And I think somebody is getting excited."

Believe me, it takes a lot to embarrass me, and it is rare that that ever happens. Well, this was one of those times. She was right. I had to admit that I *was* a little excited. I also knew that my face had to be a least fifty shades of red.

I returned to my duties and never did do a third round of drinks. Ms. Eden kept sticking her head out in the aisle, watching my every move. The experience was just a little nerve racking for me.

By the time that the plane landed, I was relieved. Well, in a way I was relived and in another was a little worried. I knew that I was going to have to help Ms. Eden off the plane. When I looked in her direction, it was clear that she knew it too. She waited for me with a sly smile.

This time I was in for another of Ms. Eden's many surprises. She didn't appear to be as helpless as she led on at first. The cane was gone as if she was now miraculously healed. She handed me her card.

"Call me as soon as you can," she said.

I am still as stunned today talking about it as I was back then. I tell you, Eden was a trip. Yes Eden…without the Ms. She insisted that I drop the Ms. after that night.

Don't judge me.

Chapter 25: This is a PSA. I'm *Not* the Baby's Daddy.

"I knew that I was an unwanted baby when I saw that my bath toys were a toaster and a radio."
–Joan Rivers

Before I get started, let me make something clear. I love kids. With that being said, you have to understand that I don't have to love *your* kids. Okay, just needed to make that perfectly clear.

I just think that it's the funniest thing when a mother and/or father comes on the plane with their very first baby. I know, I know, I understand the whole being *proud parents* issue. I get it. And oh, how some just love their little Jr. Their life is so complete now, and the universe has finally rearranged in perfect alignment. I even understand how you think you have the smartest child in the world. You are so proud of them. Yes, I get it. I have the most wonderful child in the world myself! Just the other day he came home and—wait, let me not tell that story right now. We'll save it for the next book, so stayed tuned. So, let's get back to your baby doting or drama, depending on who is listening I guess.

This lady gets on the plane with her nine month old baby. First off, she gets on the plane with a car seat, baby diaper bag, toy bag, snack bag, carry-on luggage, an over-sized purse and a *why-are-you-not-helping-me* look across her face. I returned her look with a *because-I'm-not-the-baby's-daddy* look of my own.

I hate to admit it, but I think I may have said it out loud without realizing it. I still felt for her. This poor lady moved slowly, the bags under her eyes were larger than the ones on her shoulders, and her hair was pulled back as if that's all she had the time and energy to do.

She had seen better days, I'm sure. A sloppy bun rested on the back of her head. Her shirt had more wrinkles than my elderly friend Ms.—I mean, *Eden's*—hands. On the shoulder of the shirt were multiple stains, most likely from the baby.

I could see her puff her cheeks and blow out hard. She was doing this all by herself as the little baby screamed at the top of its lungs. Before she could make eye contact with me again, I looked the other way. I pretended that I didn't see her or notice the ear splitting screams coming from the child.

Passengers avoided sitting in the area where she was headed. As she got situated, another passenger came up to me.

"Are you going to help that lady?" the Good Samaritan traveler asked.

I stared at her as if I was unfamiliar with the language she was speaking. I wanted to say, "Lady, my title is *flight attendant,* not *the super nanny.*" But instead I just gave the lady my positive smile while continuing to watch the circus.

By this time the new mom finally settled in her seat, little Helga's screams had yet to stop or even slow down. All the seats around the mom and baby were empty. No one, present company included, wanted to get close.

The flight was on its way with me seated up front. The little girl's screaming was at an all time high. A man seated three rows back had his hands cupped over his ears. Regardless of the scheduled flight time, this was going to be a *long* flight.

Soon it came time to do my drink service. There was going to be no way to avoid passing by as I made my way down the aisle. Through my years working, I'd developed a talent to block out what I didn't want to deal with, so I don't hear the screaming.

As I got to the lady with the baby, I asked her if she woul. like something to drink. Again, she had about fifty carry on bags, toys were now all over the place, and she asked for *more*.

"Can I get an apple juice, a water with lime and no ice, coffee with cream, and can you heat up the bottle?"

I gritted my teeth. *How in the hell was she going to be able to handle all this in front of her and the screaming demon at the same time?* But who am I to judge, so I granted her wishes.

When I brought her all the things she requested, she looked at me with a puzzled expression.

"Oh," she said. "I didn't want all of the drinks at the same time."

Did she realize this was an hour flight? She had no choice but to get all of this at once. If she knew what was good for her, she might want to take it now of get it *never*. The poor little screamer was still crying and couldn't sit still.

The mother decided that she was going to get up and walk the baby up and down the aisle. I understand her effort, but this drove me crazy. Midflight was *not* the time to try to entertain your baby.

Let's just be honest here. Don't get upset when I say this, but *every baby ain't cute*. There, I said it. Whew, so glad to get that out in the open. I don't know about you, but I feel better now. It needed to be said.

When she brought the baby to the back of the plane, I was standing there. Before the baby was covered up, so I could only hear her. This time I saw the baby's face and I *literally* flinched. I had never seen such an ugly baby in my entire life. I told you before, don't judge me, I'm just telling the truth.

Then the mother talked to the baby as she looked at me.

"Look at the flight attendant," she said. She said that like *I* was the monkey in the zoo and not the other way around. "Say *hi* to the flight attendant," she said, knowing damn well that this baby couldn't speak. "Ask the flight attendant for some peanuts."

I wanted to say, *Lady, if you want some more peanuts, just ask for them. Don't use Frederica the Monster to do your dirty work.* I am now wishing this lady would just go back to her seat. *Get that thing out my face...please.* Also, I know that she can smell and tell that the baby needs that diaper changed ASAP.

The baby rested on her shoulder looking right at me. I tried to avoid eyes contact.

Blaggggggh! Without warning, this baby projectile vomited breast milk all over me. Remember that scene from the exorcist? Well, yeah, this was worse. It kept coming out like an endless stream of a vile gusher. I stood, mortified and frozen in place. *That damn Linda Blair baby just threw up on me.*

"Now, doesn't that feel better?" the mother asked. She then walked away.

I was convinced that this heifer had planned the whole thing. I know that she was still mad at me for not helping her and the screaming demon to their seats.

That day I learned a spiritual lesson. It was like a glow of enlightenment fell across me, guiding me to that *ah ha* moment that Oprah always refer to as life changing. *Yes, Derrick, it is His sign...His will*, I thought to myself. *Next time I'm at the doctor's office, I'm getting a vasectomy.*

Chapter 26: Anybody Have a Tic Tac?

"Boy (boi) noun: 1. a noise with dirt on it."
– Not Your Average Dictionary

I am all for equal opportunity. If you haven't already noticed—which I seriously doubt—I just call it as I see it, with a dash of sarcasm, of course. In one of the stories I talked about a bad white kid on a flight with his mother. Well, this story is about his twin, the bad little black kid. This little ten-year-old boy was traveling alone. His trip was taking him from Baltimore to Fort Lauderdale. Yes, a long flight for a good kid, so it was infinity for a bad one.

He could not keep still for a two minute span of time. The plane turned into his playground and every item in it became his slide and or swing set. He kicked the seat in front of him non-stop. All of his snacks were poured on the floor as he talked loudly to everyone while showing little to no respect.

I worked the back of the plane so I—thank God—didn't have to deal with Satan's seed. The flight attendant up front that day was a very timid twenty-one year old white girl. The few times I did look into her section, I noticed how she avoided the kid as much as possible. My guess was that she was afraid of him.

Eventually she came to the back of the plane. Her red face fraught with worry and her blue eyes filled with heavy tears at the edge of falling down. "I…I can't control that little boy," she said. Her voice vibrated with grief. "I just don't know what to do."

Her eyes pleaded with me and she didn't have to say anything, because I knew what they were asking. *Help me...please, help me.*

"Since you are the only African American," she put it as delicately as she could manage, "could you go talk to the little boy up front?"

I guess she thought that ethnicity somehow transcended the barriers of adolescent badness. I knew better, but felt the less than wise need to flex my veteran flight attendant muscles. I got my deep, grown-man voice together, squared off my shoulders, then marched up front to confront the little boy.

I didn't have any idea that I was going to say but like always I was sure that I would come up with something. I got there in the middle of his seat kicking session. I took a deep breath then bent down to talk to him.

"You better behave," I said.

He looked at me as if I was speaking another language.

"Do you understand what I am saying to you?"

He leaned in eye to eye with me. No fear was seen in his small, black pupils. "Your breath stinks," he said.

Right then I wanted to whip his little behind. Instead of doing what I really wanted, I walked over to the phone attached near the jump seat. The phone is used to talk to the pilots and other flight attendants.

I held eye contact with him as I picked up the receiver. Instead of making an actual call, I pretended that I was calling his dad. He bought the act hands down. I scared him so bad that he returned to his seat and fell asleep.

After the plane landed in Florida, I personally walked him off the plane. His bottom lip stuck out and quivered nervously. I knew he was worried about facing his dad and I loved it.

When we got to the gate his dad was waiting there for us. The little demon seed ran to his dad and his dad gave him a warm, loving hug. The little boy's eyes shifted toward me with confusion wondering why he was getting hugged instead of scolded.

I bent down to get closer to his ear but out of range for his dad to hear me. "Now *your* breath stinks," I whispered.

Like I said, I am an equal opportunity supporter. I will get the last word end no matter what color you are, or how old.

Chapter 27: Harriet Blume

"If you enter this world knowing that you are loved and you leave the world knowing the same, then everything that happens in between can be dealt with."
–Michael Jackson

This story is dedicated to Ms. Harriet Blume. I don't really know what her real name is, so I'll just her Harriet.

This story goes back to when I was still new in my career with the airline industry. I had just become a brand new supervisor in customer service. I was only twenty-one years old, so needless to say the promotion made me feel validated and important.

As far as supervisors go, I was as new as you could possibly get. I didn't even have a supervisor uniform yet, so I wore my own fancy coat and jacket to work. I am sure that I had my little chest stuck out, feeling empowered at such a young age.

Most of the other supervisors were much older than me at the time. They had experience behind their appointed titles with ten years or more doing their jobs. I couldn't think that far ahead, since I was enamored at living in the moment.

Houston Intercontinental Airport had to be the best place to get your supervisor feet wet. It was like taking a crash course in the position since it remained busy. Something was always going on, twenty-four hours a day.

On my third day as supervisor, I worked in my zone getting accustomed to the position. I received a call over the radio that an inbound flight had an elderly lady that would need assistance off the plane.

Those were the only instructions I received. *This should be easy.* The first thing I did was call for wheel chair assistance. I also made sure that they brought me an electric cart, since I did my homework and knew that she had a close connection to another flight.

The flight pulled up to the gate and I was waiting for it. *We got action.* I donned my supervisor cape and begin making moves. Everyone was about to see that, regardless of my age, I was ready for my supervisor status.

I had no doubt that I was about to impress everybody, or should I say *show off* to everybody. I stood, fancy jacket tall, at the gate right on the edge of the jet bridge where passengers deplaned the flight. Ms. Blume was about to receive five star assistance.

The instant the door opens, I rushed onto the plane. As soon as I board, another agent came down to talk to me.

"Derrick," she urged. "Why don't you wait?"

I did not respond. I was determined to help this lady out, so I ignored the lower positioned worker. *I don't see a supervisor badge on your uniform.*

Right away, I noticed an older white lady seated in the front row. I figured that she had to be close to eighty years old. *That's her*, I thought. A younger lady, about thirty years old, was seated with her.

"Is this Ms. Blume?" I asked her.

"Yes it is," she replied. "I'm her daughter."

"Where were you guys going?" I asked. I already knew, but thought I would double check to be thorough. You know, since I *was* a supervisor.

"New Orleans," she said in a quite voice, almost as if she wasn't sure. It didn't matter, because I *was* sure and was about to make this happen.

I got the wheel chair attendant to help me get Ms. Blume into the wheel chair. The plan was to move her as fast as possible onto the electric cart and rush to her connecting gate.

Everyone around me tried to take me off focus.

"Derrick…Derrick," someone said. "Why don't you wait until everyone is off the plane?"

I remained set on proving myself. Completing this simply task was my *only* focus. I pushed Ms. Blume up the jet bridge into the gate area. We tired to put Ms. Blume onto to electric cart. She was too heavy, but she looked like she weighed a buck fifty.

Okay, plan B. I though that I would just push her to the connecting gate myself. I slung the two bags on my shoulder, and with the daughter by my side, we hurried off. *When there is a will there is a way, right?*

It was not easy. While I pushed Ms. Blume, she kept sliding out the wheelchair. I stopped, scooped her back up in the chair, and then continued. "Ms. Blume, you have to sit up now so I can get you to the gate," I said while moving through the airport.

We hit a rubber bump and there went Ms. Blume. Her wide body slumped down in the wheelchair and almost fell out. I pulled her back up. "Ms. Blume," I said as politely as possible. "You've got to help me out. Sit up, okay? We're almost there."

Meanwhile, the daughter was still right on my heels. After an exhausting run, I got to the other gate.

"Okay Ms. Blume," I said out of breath. "You need to get on your connecting flight now."

The gate agent was already waiting for me. I was relieved that someone had called her to tell her that I was on my way. She walked past Ms. Blume and pulled me to the side. "She's not with us," she said.

The words went right over my head. "Yes, she is. I already checked," I said. "Now let's get her on the plane."

"Derrick," she said. "She is *not with us.*"

At this time I saw red lights flashing outside. Paramedics appeared as they came from running up the stairs.

"They were at the other gate," the agent explained. "But because *you* took Ms. Blume away from there to here, they had to drive around to the other side of the airport."

When they got to the top of the stairs they rushed over to Ms. Blume. "Clear!" One of the paramedics yelled out as the other placed the hand held small metal plates against her chest.

My mouth would not close as I stared in total astonishment.

Soon, Ms. Blume was on the floor. The paramedics perfumed CPR on her, followed by another round of the shock treatments.

What the hell?

"Derrick, everyone tired to tell you before you left the gate. Ms. Blume is dead," the agent said.

I stood there, unable to move. It hit me like a bad dream. *I had just pushed a dead lady around the whole airport.*

You may have thought otherwise, but I am not one of those who think that I know it all. Lord knows that I don't, but I do know this—I know Ms. Blume was looking down at me at that time saying, "Now *you* go sit your dumb ass down!"

Epilogue

"The guardian angels of life fly so high as to be beyond our sight, but they are always looking down upon us."
–Paul Richter

When I think back about that first flight so many years ago, I smile every single time. It is engrained in my memory as one of those special moments that I will never forget. I think about how my grandmother felt confident with me by her side when we flew across the country and I never once wondered why she needed company.

That is the beauty of seeing life through the eyes of a child—you enjoy the moments. I recall feeling so honored to fly with her and even excited to know that I would be flying back alone. We sat side by side as I wore that little suite I mentioned and a permanent grin, feeling beyond special.

As my tiny eyes peered out of the oval window through those thick black glasses, I felt empowered. *I could do anything.* For that particular moment all those years ago, I was on a mission determined to find those angels.

Back then I savored the moment. I thought it was a one in a lifetime experience, but unknown to me, it was just the first of countless flights to come. Now I fly all the time and watch how the other new flight attendants have the same wide-eyed excitement I had at thirteen years old.

One day I worked a trip with a brand new flight attendant. She was in her early twenties and this was her first major job. Her name was Lori and she had worked a stint as a professional NFL cheerleader.

She floated through the cabin and skipped down the aisle with the demeanor of a pageant queen. Her walk, talk, and even over-abundant smile had a way of grinding against my nerves. And not just the last nerve, but even ones that I hadn't even received yet were pushed to the edge.

I tried not to be too hard on her. I chalked it up to being brand new. Far be it for me to steal her joy. Yet, it was that look-at-me attitude that I found hard to deal with.

Lori was one of those flight attendants that demanded everybody's attention. She was not happy unless all eyes were on her. When she wasn't the center of attention, something had to be wrong with *you*. The happy demeanor fell short when it came to the job.

No matter how much training some of the airline attendants receive, most still have no idea what it takes to do this job. Sooner or later the job and/or passengers—just like it did with me—take a toll on you. What amazed me though, was that it was only Lori's third flight before she started complaining about working for the airline.

You could have sworn that she had been on the job for years and ready for retirement. Lord help those when its time for my retirement. You think I let things slip off my tongue now…can you just imagine my last day? Believe me, I won't be like the flight attendant that opened a can of beer and jumped on the emergency slide. I'm going to do it big. I'm going to be spilling drinks on folks, cussing folks out, and, hold on…I'm not going to tell everything I'm going to do. Can't ruin the surprise.

Anyway, so Lori was whining about everything. Her pay, the hours, and being away from home were already eating at her. Like I said, when you apply to work for an airline, you know from the beginning what is required from you. There are no secrets about what the job is all about.

We were on are way to Fort Lauderdale and the weather was going to be a cloudless seventy-five degrees. Thoughts of slipping on my flip flops, swim suit, and heading to the beach were all that my mind would allow me to focus on that day. As soon as we landed, we gathered our things and headed to the hotel.

Lori still complained about whatever she could find. My head remained turned and gazing out the window, acting as if I can't hear her. I'm pretty good at tuning out people when necessary.

Once we landed, my relaxation plan went into action. I changed out of the uniform and into my beach gear. As I was relaxing on the beach, a dark cloud approached, but it wasn't in the clear Florida skies. Here came Lori.

She moved in my direction, turning a few heads in the process. Surprisingly enough, her petite but shapely little body dawned a tattoo that came out her two-piece swimsuit with belly rings. My guess was that she purchased the swimsuit at the age of three and was determined to *never* stop wearing it.

I prayed for someone, anyone, to hurry up and bury me in the sand. No luck, she spotted me. The very second that she sat down, she started complaining about the job. I rolled my eyes beneath my sunglasses.

It was time for an intervention. I had to stop her so I could go through a period of meditation. "Lori," I said removing my glasses. "Look out in the water and tell me what you see."

"Boats, water, and ships," she said.

"And what do you see sitting around us?"

She rotated her head in every direction. "People?"

"Right. And how many people do you believe spent money, a *lot* of money, to take a trip out here?"

"At least ninety percent. So what's your point?"

"My point is, flight attendants are able to travel all over the world. We could sit on the beach until the sun goes down if we wanted. What other job could you go to and get *paid* while sitting on the beach?"

I placed my shades back on, leaned into the beach chair, and returned to my peaceful meditation. Out of the corner of my eye, I watched Lori do the same. *I think she got it.*

In all honesty, the words hit me at the same time as they hit her. I realized something at that very instant—*I was very thankful for my job.* My travels, fellow flight attendants, and even my passengers have created some special moments for me. Without our passengers I wouldn't have the stories I was able to tell you today, and to be honest, I look forward to going to work and getting more.

On that first flight with my grandmother over three decades ago, I got it. Somehow through the years, life has a way of dulling our senses. Then, I enjoyed the moment. Like I said, I was never scared, just curious.

As I stared out the window, the entire time looking for those angels, my Grandmother asked if I was okay. She noticed my far away gaze and picked up on my distraction.

"I'm just looking," I said in my squeaky voice.

About a year after that flight, my grandmother passed away. I had no idea at the time that she had cancer and was flying to California to spend her finals days with family there. Like I said, I never did get to see any angels. Yet, even today, every now and then I catch myself leaning down to take a peak out of one of the airplane's windows.

Deep down that same belief is still there. *They're moving out of the way again. That's why I didn't see them.* It would be so nicc to scc onc, but I don't have to, because I now know what they look like and what they are doing up there. They look like my grandmother, MiMi, with those big beautiful brown eyes and they are there watching over me.

"I give my best customer service when my mouth is shut!"
–Derrick Dixon

Thank you to Carl Henegan. It's amazing when GOD does his work and when you have true friends, they are friends for life.

Thank you to my co-workers for letting me be myself, and a special thanks to my wonderful mother for your support and love.

To MaryJo Brezzell, thank you for always believing in me and teaching me to live life. I know you are smiling down on me.

To Kelly Brezzell Guster, thank you for showing me so much love and support. I am waiting for your book.

To Kim Thomas, thank you for just for being you.

I want to thank all the passengers that have helped make this all possible. We have to learn to laugh and laugh at ourselves. Some people will think I was making fun of them, and that's okay, *I was,* but it was done all out of fun, laughter, and love.

Before you ask, *yes,* I'm working on another book!

17840460R00062

Made in the USA
Charleston, SC
03 March 2013